The One-Pot Gourmet

The One-Pot Gourmet

125 Simply Delicious Dinners

Pat Dailey

LARK BOOKS

A Division of
Sterling Publishing Co., Inc.
New York

Library of Congress Cataloging-in-Publication Data

Dailey, Pat.
   The one-pot gourmet : 125 simply delicious dinners / Pat Dailey.— 1st ed.
      p. cm.
   Originally published: One pot Sunday suppers. New York : HarpersCollins,
1996.
   Includes index.
   ISBN 1-57990-647-8 (hardcover)
   1. Casserole cookery. I. Dailey, Pat. One pot Sunday suppers. II. Title.
TX693.D28 2005
641.8'21—dc22
                                            2004015557

First Edition

Published by Lark Books, A Division of
Sterling Publishing Co., Inc.
387 Park Avenue South, New York, N.Y. 10016

© 2005, John Boswell Management, Inc. and King Hill Productions

Distributed in Canada by Sterling Publishing,
c/o Canadian Manda Group, 165 Dufferin Street
Toronto, Ontario, Canada M6K 3H6

Distributed in the U.K. by Guild of Master Craftsman Publications Ltd.,
Castle Place, 166 High Street, Lewes, East Sussex, England BN7 1XU
Tel: (+ 44) 1273 477374, Fax: (+ 44) 1273 478606,
Email: pubs@thegmcgroup.com, Web: www.gmcpublications.com

Distributed in Australia by Capricorn Link (Australia) Pty Ltd.,
P.O. Box 704, Windsor, NSW 2756 Australia

Originally published as *One Pot Sunday Suppers* in 1996 by
Harper Collins Publishers.

If you have questions or comments about this book, please contact:
Lark Books
67 Broadway
Asheville, NC 28801
(828) 253-0467

Manufactured in China

ISBN 1-57990-647-8

EDITOR:
Marthe Le Van

ART DIRECTOR:
Kristi Pfeffer

COVER DESIGNER:
Barbara Zaretsky

ILLUSTRATIONS:
Lance Wille

ASSISTANT EDITOR:
Nathalie Mornu, Susan Kieffer

EDITORIAL ASSISTANCE:
Delores Gosnell

EDITORIAL INTERN:
Janna Norton, Matthew M. Paden

ASSOCIATE ART DIRECTOR:
Lance Wille, Shannon Yokeley

Contents

52 Dinner's in the Oven

Chicken & Turkey 70 for Dinner

Introduction

You can prepare amazing meals without spending all your time in the kitchen. The best—and easiest—way to do so is to become a one-pot gourmet. With this approach you cook a single interesting and exotic dish that becomes the centerpiece of a memorable meal. In *The One-Pot Gourmet* you'll discover 125 simple and simply delicious ways to serve up abundance, hospitality, and good taste. With these recipes, you can reap the pleasures and rewards of an uncomplicated yet delicious meal.

Dinner doesn't have to be a multi-course affair. Grand as this type of feast may seem, it speaks of another era. Today, most people choose meals that are more healthy, ethnically diverse, and exciting. The contemporary recipes in this book joyously reflect these changes. Meat and potatoes are still featured, but they're combined in different proportions, favoring lighter, more vibrant ingredients. Grains, beans, and pastas augment meat and poultry and sometimes displace them altogether. Fish has become a welcome, healthy addition to the mealtime repertoire. And sturdy, meal-in-a-bowl soups sometimes steal the whole show. Whatever form a one-pot meal takes, it can nurture you, your friends, and family without compromising time or nutrition for taste.

In these recipes, you'll find gourmet options to fit any mood or season. Lentil & Sausage Soup with Feta & Mint can take the chill off a winter's night, while Scallops with Corn, Bacon & Tomatoes celebrates summer's harvest. Ethnic influences abound in the likes of Sao Paulo Seafood Stew, Malaysian Vegetable Stew with Gingery Coconut Milk, and the sensational African Bobotie. Pasta with Chicken, Greens & Herbed Chicken and Pony's Cowpoke Pintos make terrific pot-luck dishes, while the Rack of Lamb with Couscous, Roasted Fennel & Peppers, and Potato & Celery Root Soup with Apples & Smoked Trout are perfect for more intimate, special occasion dining.

The concept of one-pot suggests an inherent and much-needed simplicity and, indeed, most of the recipes are straightforward. For convenience, there is some reliance on canned foods, mostly in the form of broths, tomato products, chipotle chilies, coconut milk, and beans. Cooking dried beans is usually preferable but requires planning. To help manage your schedule in this respect, each recipe comes with an approximate start-to-finish cooking time, including how long it will take to prep, soak, or marinate the ingredients.

A well-stocked condiment cabinet is a boon to the one-pot gourmet. Vinegars, mustards, Thai seasonings, and lots of herbs and spices do wonders for dishes. As you survey the ingredient lists and prepare meals, you'll develop a feel for what staples are most practical to keep in stock. In most cases, there are also alternative suggestions for ingredients that may be hard to locate or that are seasonal. Extra tips for finding and using less common ingredients are included; you can identify these hints by their common heading, "FYI." And, if fresh tomatoes are in season, chicken breasts are on sale, or you receive a bushel of homegrown peppers, the ingredient index at the back of the book will help you make the most of your good fortune and turn your windfall into a one-pot meal.

The more dedicated you become to one-pot cooking, the more you'll find yourself looking for pots and pans that match this style. Several casseroles and a good-sized roasting pan are key. Those that are flameproof often eliminate the need to wash extra pots as they can be transferred directly from the stovetop to the oven. A straight-sided sauté pan is very versatile. Similar to a skillet, the straight, deeper sides mean they hold more. Many are ovenproof, making them even more useful. One-pot cooking also means cleaning up is less of a chore. And many of the meals can be served in the same pan you've cooked them in, which means more time for you to relax after dinner and appreciate your one-pot gourmet meal.

Move over, dinner plates—make room for bowls. Dinner now comes to the table in big, heaping, filled-to-the-brim dishes. Soups are now apt to include a broader spectrum of deliciously sustaining possibilities, from chili to chowder to gumbo. Even the vessels they're served in reflect their new, starring-role status. Once small and barely able to contain a whole meal, soup bowls have grown up in size and stature, all the better to hold enough to satisfy any appetite.

Almost without exception, dinners that are self-contained meals-in-a-bowl are simple and require little fuss; they are perfectly suited to casual and free-spirited meals. **Chickpea & Tomato Soup** is fragrant, filling, cooked in a flash, and made to order for those perfect autumn days when it's hard to be indoors. **Bean & Barley Soup** offers sturdy substance, a warming buffer to wintry days. **St. Peter Street Seafood & Sausage Gumbo** is bold and sassy, ideally suited for entertaining. **Onion Soup Olé** is a slightly irreverent, completely satisfying pairing of French tradition and Tex-Mex tastes.

Dinner in a Bowl: Soups, Chilis & Gumbos

Soups, chilis, and gumbos graciously accept impromptu changes and innovations based on what the market offers or what you happen to like. One vegetable easily can be swapped for another, meats added or omitted, and herbs varied by whim or by will. Many of the recipes can be made ahead of time and reheated, a big boon to busy weeknight schedules. Even freezing is a possibility, so the work can be done on a lazy stay-at-home day, and the rewards reaped as necessary. Making double batches is often a good idea, adding little more to the workload, but paying off handsomely when they're turned into frozen assets.

Bread is often essential to round out dinners that are served in a bowl. Match the bread to the menu, selecting from Italian-style flatbreads, flaky biscuits, rustic country loaves, warm cornbread, or even toasted pita bread. Depending on appetites, a salad or fresh vegetable relish also can be added.

Chickpea & Tomato Soup

Despite a simple list of ingredients and a straightforward presentation, this soup is loaded with charm and home-style appeal. If you use canned chickpeas, almost no advance planning is required, and the soup can be table-ready with very little effort. If time allows, homemade croutons add a nice final flourish.

MAKES:
4 servings

PREP:
10 minutes

COOK:
40 minutes

1 In a large saucepan, heat the oil over medium heat. Add the garlic, onion, and hot pepper. Cook, stirring often, until the onion is softened but not browned, about 5 minutes.

2 Add the tomatoes with their juices, the vinegar, and rosemary. Increase the heat to high and boil until juice from the tomatoes thickens, about 5 minutes.

3 Add the chickpeas, chicken stock, and salt. Cover and simmer 30 minutes, stirring occasionally and smashing some of the beans with the back of a spoon. To serve, sprinkle with the cheese and the croutons.

3   **tablespoons olive oil**

3   **large garlic cloves, minced**

1   **small onion, minced**

¼   **teaspoon crushed hot red pepper**

1   **(14½-ounce) can diced tomatoes, juices reserved**

1   **tablespoon balsamic vinegar**

1   **teaspoon dried rosemary**

2   **cups cooked chickpeas (garbanzo beans) or 1 (16-ounce) can chickpeas, rinsed and drained**

4   **cups chicken stock or reduced-sodium canned broth**

¼   **teaspoon salt, or to taste**

½   **cup grated Parmesan cheese**

½   **cup croutons**

St. Peter Street Seafood & Sausage Gumbo

Gumbo, one of the great glories of Cajun cooking, is completely forthright in its many charms, and big flavors abound. It's surprisingly easy to make, although a certain amount of attention must be paid to making the roux. Use a heavy pan—flimsy ones just won't do; get the oil hot before the flour is added and stir it constantly as it cooks. Be careful when cooking the roux and adding the vegetables to it because it gets very hot.

MAKES:
6 servings

PREP:
30 minutes

COOK:
1 hour, 10 minutes

½   cup vegetable oil

½   pound okra, cut into ½-inch-thick slices

6   tablespoons flour

1   red bell pepper, cut into ½-inch dice

1   green bell pepper, cut into ½-inch dice

1   large onion, finely diced

2   medium celery ribs, finely diced

2   garlic cloves, minced

2   small tomatoes, peeled, seeded, and diced

5   cups fish stock or clam juice

2   bay leaves

2   tablespoons Cajun seasoning blend

½   teaspoon salt

½   teaspoon ground black pepper

8 to 10   ounces andouille sausage, sliced ½ inch thick

1   pound peeled large shrimp

1   pound lump crabmeat

3   tablespoons minced parsley

Hot red pepper sauce

1 In a large, heavy soup pot, heat 2 tablespoons of the oil. Add the okra, reduce the heat to low, and cook until the okra is very soft, about 25 minutes. Remove the okra from the pan and set aside.

2 To make the roux, wipe out the pan with a paper towel. Add the remaining oil and set over medium-high heat. When the oil is very hot, gradually add the flour, whisking constantly. Switch to a wooden spoon and cook, stirring constantly, until the roux takes on a rich, medium-dark brown color, 3 to 5 minutes. (Watch carefully that the roux doesn't burn.) Carefully stir in the bell peppers, onion, and celery. Reduce the heat to medium-low and cook, stirring occasionally, until the vegetables begin to soften, about 5 minutes. Add the garlic and stir 30 seconds.

3 Add the okra, tomatoes, fish stock, bay leaves, and seasonings. Bring to a boil. Reduce the heat to low and simmer gently 30 minutes. Add the sausage, shrimp, and crabmeat. Cook just until the shrimp are pink and curled, 3 to 5 minutes. Remove and discard the bay leaves. Stir in the parsley. Season with hot sauce to taste.

From South Louisiana comes spicy, heavily smoked **andouille sausage**. A specialty of Cajun cooking, andouille is traditionally used in jambalaya and gumbo. Made with coarse-ground pork and seasoned with salt, black pepper, and garlic, this sausage is stuffed into beef casing, and then slowly smoked over pecan wood and sugar cane until it becomes very dark in color.

If you already have the spices, you can mix up your own batch of **Creole seasoning** in a flash.

2 tablespoons ground cayenne

2 tablespoons black pepper

4 tablespoons paprika

1 teaspoon dried thyme

1 teaspoon dried oregano

½ tablespoon garlic powder

1 teaspoon onion powder

2 tablespoons salt

Place all the ingredients in a jar and shake well.

Yucatán-Style Chicken Soup with Poblano Pepper & Lime

This is a deceptively simple recipe, but the resulting soup, redolent of garlic and suffused with smoky undertones, is a delightful surprise. Putting leftover chicken, or any type of poultry, to use here makes the preparation streamlined and quick. If you don't wish to add the fried tortilla strips, you can pass warm tortillas at the table.

MAKES:
3 to 4 servings

PREP:
15 minutes

COOK:
35 minutes

3	**medium tomatoes**
4	**large garlic cloves, unpeeled**
1	**poblano pepper**
5	**cups chicken stock or reduced-sodium canned broth**
2	**tablespoons chopped cilantro**
1	**jalapeño pepper, sliced**
	Pinch of dried oregano
1½	**cups shredded cooked chicken**
2	**scallions, thinly sliced**
	Fried corn tortilla strips (optional)
1	**lime, cut into wedges**

1 Put the tomatoes, garlic, and poblano pepper in a dry cast-iron skillet. Cook over high heat until the skins are blackened, turning them often and removing each item when it is fully charred, 12 to 15 minutes in all. Transfer the poblano to a small paper bag, close tightly, and set aside for 10 minutes.

2 Peel and chop the garlic. Then, using the flat side of a large knife, smash it into a paste. Transfer to a large nonreactive saucepan. Chop the tomatoes and add to the pan with the chicken stock, cilantro, jalapeño pepper, and oregano. Cover and bring to a boil; reduce the heat to low and simmer gently 10 minutes.

3 Peel the blackened skin from the poblano pepper; remove the core and seeds. Cut the pepper into ½-inch squares. Add to the pan along with the chicken and scallions. Cook 2 minutes longer. Serve topped with tortilla strips, if desired, and a lime wedge.

Bean & Barley Soup

Use your favorite beans here—as many different types as you can rustle up. Try for red and white kidney beans, navy, black, pinto, black-eyed peas, yellow-eyes, and Great Northerns. It is all the more fun and interesting to mix up a varied pot.

MAKES:
8 to 10 servings

SOAK:
12 hours or overnight

PREP:
15 minutes

COOK:
3 hours

1 Place the beans in a large soup pot and add enough cold water to cover by at least 2 inches. Soak 12 hours or overnight. Drain the beans into a colander and rinse under cold running water.

2 In the same pot, combine the soaked beans with 6 cups water, the ham bone, barley, bay leaves, and rosemary. Cover and bring to a boil. Reduce the heat to low and simmer gently 2 hours.

3 Add the onion, celery, carrots, tomatoes with their juices, salt, pepper, and cumin. Cook, uncovered, until the vegetables are tender and the soup has thickened slightly, about 1 hour. Remove the ham bone and cut the meat into bite-size pieces. Remove and discard the bay leaves. Return the meat to the soup and add additional salt and pepper as needed. Stir in the vinegar just before serving.

2 **cups dried beans, rinsed and picked over**

1 **ham bone or smoked ham hock**
3 **tablespoons pearl barley**
3 **bay leaves**
1 **teaspoon dried rosemary**

1 **large onion, diced**
3 **large celery ribs, diced**
3 **large carrots, peeled and diced**
1 **(14½-ounce) can diced tomatoes, juices reserved**
2 **teaspoons salt**
2 **teaspoons coarsely cracked black pepper**
1 **teaspoon ground cumin**

1 **tablespoon balsamic or red wine vinegar**

Tuscan Bread & Vegetable Soup

Throughout Tuscany, ribollita, *which means "re-boiled" in Italian, is a revered soup. It's thick, soothing, and utterly delicious.*

MAKES:
6 servings

PREP:
20 minutes

COOK:
2 hours, 15 minutes

REFRIGERATE:
overnight

REHEAT:
10 minutes

¼   cup olive oil

2   ounces pancetta, finely diced, or ½ cup diced bacon

1   medium red onion, chopped

2   celery ribs, chopped

1   carrot, peeled and chopped

2   large garlic cloves, minced

½   of a small head of Savoy or green cabbage, shredded

1   small bunch of Swiss chard, sliced

1   large Idaho potato, peeled and cut into 1-inch cubes

¼   teaspoon salt

¼   teaspoon freshly ground pepper

6   cups chicken stock or reduced-sodium canned chicken or vegetable broth

2   tablespoons tomato paste

¾   teaspoon dried thyme leaves

1   (16-ounce) can cannellini beans, rinsed and drained

8   ounces Italian bread, cut into 8 slices

Extra virgin olive oil

1. In a large heavy saucepan, heat the olive oil over medium heat. Add the pancetta and cook, stirring occasionally, until lightly browned, 3 to 4 minutes.

2. Add the red onion, celery, carrot, and garlic. Cook until the vegetables begin to brown at the edges, 12 to 15 minutes. Add the cabbage, chard, potato, salt, and pepper. Cook, stirring often, until the greens are wilted, 6 to 8 minutes.

3. Add the chicken stock, tomato paste, and thyme. Cover and bring to a boil. Reduce the heat to low and simmer gently 1¾ hours.

4. Add the beans and cook 5 minutes. Add the bread, arranging the slices in layers, pressing some down to the bottom of the pot and interspersing the rest throughout. Cover and refrigerate overnight.

5. At serving time, reheat gently, adding additional stock and salt and pepper if needed. Pass a cruet of olive oil at the table.

Pancetta is an Italian-style bacon with a mild, spicy-sweet flavor. Most often, it's cured with salt and pepper rather than smoked. Pancetta is sold flat or rolled into a sausage shape. If necessary, you could substitute prosciutto, equal parts prosciutto and salt pork, or unsmoked lean bacon.

A member of the beet family but lacking a bulb, **Swiss chard** is a large leafy green vegetable with pronounced white or red stalks. It has very tasty and good-looking crinkly green leaves. You can use chard much like spinach, except its heavier texture requires longer cooking. By adding thinly sliced chard stems and leaves during the final moments of cooking, you can liven up many soups and stews.

A traditional white Italian bean, the **cannellini** is oval, smooth, and thin-skinned with an elusive nutty flavor. Also known as white kidney or fazolia beans, cannellinis are available dried and canned. If you can't find cannellini beans, substitute Great Northern beans or white navy beans.

Wild Rice, Mushroom & Barley Soup with Smoked Chicken

MAKES:
4 to 6 servings

PREP:
25 minutes

COOK:
1 hour

Wild rice and chicken long have been companions in the soup pot, but there's ample room for exploring new ways to invigorate the relationship. Smoked chicken adds an intense backdrop for the rice, which is joined here by chewy little bits of barley.

2	tablespoons unsalted butter
1	small onion, chopped
1	small leek (white and tender green), chopped
2	small carrots, peeled and sliced
2	small celery ribs, finely diced
1	teaspoon dried thyme leaves
5½	cups chicken stock or reduced-sodium canned broth
½	cup wild rice
¼	cup barley
¼	pound fresh mushrooms, morels if available, or Italian brown (cremini), sliced
¼	cup dry sherry
1½	cups smoked chicken, shredded
2	tablespoons flour
½	cup heavy cream
¼	teaspoon salt, or to taste
⅛	teaspoon freshly ground pepper

1 In a large saucepan, melt the butter over medium-high heat. Add the onion, leek, carrots, celery, and thyme. Cook, stirring often, until the leek and onion are tender, about 5 minutes. Add the chicken stock, wild rice, and barley and bring to a boil. Reduce the heat to medium-low, cover, and simmer gently until the rice is almost tender, about 45 minutes.

2 Add the mushrooms, sherry, and smoked chicken. Cook until the wild rice is tender, 10 to 15 minutes longer. Blend the flour with 2 tablespoons cold water to make a smooth paste. Mix about ½ cup of the broth from the soup into the flour mixture. Whisking as you do so, add the flour mixture to the soup along with the cream, salt, and pepper. Bring to a boil, stirring until thickened, 3 to 4 minutes. Serve hot.

Crab, Shrimp & Corn Chowder

An indulgently rich New England-style corn chowder, with the requisite bounty of fresh seafood, takes a tasty turn to the Southwest when it becomes acquainted with Mexican ingredients.

MAKES:
3 to 4 servings
PREP:
15 minutes
COOK:
30 minutes

1 In a large saucepan, melt 1½ tablespoons of the butter. Add the onion and garlic. Cook over medium heat, stirring often, until the onion is softened but not browned, about 5 minutes. Transfer to a blender. Add the corn, fish stock, and cornstarch, and puree until smooth.

2 Melt the remaining 1½ tablespoons butter in the same pan over medium heat. Add the corn puree and cook, stirring often, until the mixture thickens, 4 to 5 minutes. Add the milk and heat to a simmer. Cover partially and simmer gently 10 minutes.

3 Strain the soup through a fine strainer, pressing the solids to release as much liquid as possible. Return the strained soup to the pan and add the crabmeat, shrimp, cream, poblano peppers, chipotle pepper, and salt. Heat just to a simmer. Serve hot, garnished with lime slices and cilantro.

3 **tablespoons unsalted butter**
1 **medium onion, chopped**
1 **small garlic clove, minced**

3 **cups corn kernels (from 3 to 4 ears)**
¼ **cup fish stock or water**
1½ **tablespoons cornstarch**

2 **cups milk**

1 **cup lump crabmeat (4 to 5 ounces)**
¼ **pound cooked peeled medium shrimp**
1 **cup heavy cream**
2 **poblano or Anaheim peppers, roasted and diced, or 1 (7-ounce) can diced roasted chilies**
1 **canned chipotle pepper, finely minced (optional)**
½ **teaspoon salt, or to taste**

3 to 4 **lime slices**
Chopped fresh cilantro

Tohatchi Two-Bean Chili

Ask 10 people what makes the best chili, and there are likely to be 12 answers. Chili prompts endless debates, even cook-offs, in attempts to settle the age-old question of which is the best. Depends on whom you ask. But this chili has a lot going for it, including two kinds of meat and beans and a spiciness that's anything but shy.

MAKES:
8 servings

PREP:
15 minutes

COOK:
45 minutes

1½ pounds coarsely ground beef chuck

½ pound coarsely ground pork

2 large onions, chopped

2 large garlic cloves, minced

1 large red bell pepper, cut into ½-inch dice

1 large green bell pepper, cut into ½-inch dice

1 cup beef stock or reduced-sodium canned broth

1 (28-ounce) can plum tomatoes, coarsely crushed, with their juices

1 (6-ounce) can tomato paste

½ cup chopped pickled jalapeño peppers

¼ cup chili powder

2 tablespoons brown sugar

2 teaspoons ground cumin

¾ teaspoon salt, or to taste

¼ teaspoon cayenne

1 (15-ounce) can pinto beans, rinsed and drained

1 (16-ounce) can kidney beans, rinsed and drained

½ cup sour cream

1 cup shredded Cheddar cheese

1 In a large soup pot, cook the ground meats over medium heat, stirring occasionally, until evenly browned, 8 to 10 minutes. Add the onions and garlic and cook until the onions are softened, about 5 minutes.

2 Add the red and green bell peppers, beef stock, tomatoes with their juices, tomato paste, jalapeño peppers, chili powder, brown sugar, cumin, salt, and cayenne. Cook, uncovered, stirring occasionally, until slightly thickened, 25 to 30 minutes, watching closely so the mixture doesn't burn.

3 Add the beans and cook 5 minutes. Adjust the seasoning and serve topped with a dollop of sour cream and a generous sprinkling of cheese.

Lentil & Sausage Soup with Feta & Mint

With an earthy, peppery taste that is endlessly comforting, lentils seem perfectly suited to the soup pot. Many ingredients are flattered by their presence, from humble sausages to the most delicate of greens and herbs.

MAKES:
6 servings

PREP:
15 minutes

COOK:
50 minutes

1 In a large soup pot, cook the sausage over medium-high heat, stirring occasionally, until evenly browned, 6 to 7 minutes. Drain off excess fat. Add the onions and celery to the pan and cook, stirring often, until the onions are softened, 6 to 8 minutes.

2 Add the lentils, 8 cups of the chicken stock, the tomatoes with their juices, and the wine. Cover partially and cook until the lentils are tender but still hold their shape, about 35 minutes. Add the remaining chicken stock if the soup is too thick.

3 Add the chard and cook just until it wilts, about 2 minutes. Remove from the heat and stir in the mint. Season with salt and pepper to taste and serve sprinkled with cheese.

1   **pound hot Italian sausage, casings removed, crumbled**

2   **medium onions, chopped**

3   **celery ribs, chopped**

1¾   **cups lentils**

8 to 10   **cups chicken stock or reduced-sodium canned broth**

2   **(14½-ounce) cans diced tomatoes, juices reserved**

1   **cup dry red wine**

1   **pound red or green Swiss chard, cut into 1-inch ribbons**

⅓   **cup chopped fresh mint**
     Salt and freshly ground pepper

¾   **cup crumbled feta cheese**

Big Red Chili

"Big" describes the taste and the attitude of this spunky, spicy chili. It's closest to Texas-style chili, since it's made without beans, but by all means, stir some in if you're so inclined. Purists, who insist that beans never mingle with the meat, might balk, but it won't be the first time it's been done.

MAKES:
6 to 8 servings

PREP:
15 minutes

COOK:
2 hours, 30 minutes

2 teaspoons cumin seeds

3 tablespoons vegetable oil

2½ pounds beef chuck, cut into ¾-inch cubes

2 medium onions, chopped

3 garlic cloves, minced

2 jalapeño peppers, minced

¼ cup chili powder

2 tablespoons pure ground New Mexican chili (optional)

1 (28-ounce) can crushed tomatoes

1 cup beef stock or reduced-sodium canned broth

1 teaspoon ground coriander

½ teaspoon dried oregano

¾ teaspoon salt

1 In a large pot, cook the cumin seeds over medium heat, shaking the pan often, until the seeds are toasted and fragrant, 2 to 3 minutes. Remove the seeds from the pan and grind in a spice grinder or with a mortar and pestle.

2 Heat half of the oil in the same pot over high heat. Add half of the meat and cook, turning occasionally, until browned on all sides, 8 to 10 minutes. Set the meat aside. Repeat with the remaining oil and meat.

3 Add the onions, garlic, and jalapeño peppers to the same pan. Cook, stirring often, until they begin to soften, 3 to 4 minutes. Add the chili powder and ground chile. Cook, stirring, for 30 seconds.

4 Add the meat, tomatoes, beef stock, coriander, oregano, ground toasted cumin, and salt. Cover and simmer gently until the meat is tender, 2 to 2½ hours; add additional beef stock or water if the mixture seems dry. Season with additional salt to taste before serving.

Potato & Celery Root Soup with Apples & Smoked Trout

This soothing soup has both rustic and refined traits. The potatoes lend body and their characteristic sturdiness, while the celery root suggests a delicate hint of celery. Apple adds its snap, while bacon and smoked trout add a smoky, woodsy taste.

MAKES:
3 to 4 servings
PREP:
25 minutes
COOK:
40 minutes

1 In a large saucepan, cook the bacon until crisp. Drain on a paper towel. Add the onion to the drippings in the saucepan and cook, stirring often, until the onion begins to soften, 4 to 5 minutes.

2 Add the potatoes, celery root, apple, 3 cups of the chicken stock, the thyme, and ⅓ cup of the flaked trout. Cover and bring to a boil. Reduce the heat to low and simmer gently until the vegetables are very soft, 20 to 25 minutes.

3 Strain the solids from the broth, reserving both. Puree the solids in a food processor or blender until smooth. Stir a small amount of the broth into the puree. Pour the puree back into the remaining broth in the saucepan and add the salt, pepper, and cream. If the soup is too thick, add the remaining 1 cup chicken stock. Garnish with the remaining trout and chives.

2 **bacon slices, diced**

1 **medium onion, diced**

2 **medium yellow or red potatoes, peeled and sliced**

1 **medium celery root, peeled and sliced**

1 **small tart apple, peeled, cored, and sliced**

3 to 4 **cups chicken stock or reduced-sodium canned broth**

1 **teaspoon fresh thyme leaves or ½ teaspoon dried**

1 **small side smoked rainbow trout, skinned and flaked (about 1 cup)**

¼ **teaspoon salt, or to taste**

⅛ **teaspoon freshly ground pepper**

½ **cup heavy cream**

Fresh chives, minced

Mongolian Fire Pot with Beef & Shrimp

Throughout China, intricate cooking vessels called fire pots are put to use for regional variants on the classic Mongolian fire pot that uses lamb as the centerpiece for communal cooking. Various meats and vegetables, cut into bite-size pieces, are dipped by diners first into simmering broth, then into a flavorful dipping sauce. The boiling stock gets tastier with each addition, and what remains after all the food has been cooked is then eaten as soup. Practicality suggests adapting the recipe to a hot plate or the stovetop. Although it's somewhat less dramatic than when the fire pot stands at the center of the table, it still has the same convivial feel.

MAKES:
6 servings

PREP:
25 minutes

COOK:
30 minutes

¾ cup soy sauce

¼ cup plus 3 tablespoons rice wine or dry sherry

2 tablespoons seasoned rice vinegar

½ teaspoon sugar

½ teaspoon hot chili oil

7 scallions, 1 minced and 6 cut into 2-inch lengths

¾ teaspoon minced fresh ginger

3 small garlic cloves, minced

1 pound beef tenderloin or top sirloin, cut into paper-thin slices

1 teaspoon Asian sesame oil

Pinch of crushed hot red pepper

1 pound shrimp, peeled and deveined, with the tails left intact

½ pound extra firm tofu, cut into squares (optional)

½ pound small fresh shiitake mushrooms, stemmed

2 carrots, peeled and julienned or shredded

½ pound Chinese greens, such as pea tops, bok choy, or spinach

2 tablespoons peanut or vegetable oil

1 pound Chinese cabbage, cut into 2-inch squares

6 cups chicken stock or reduced-sodium canned broth

¾ teaspoon salt, or to taste

1. For the dipping sauce, combine ½ cup plus 2 tablespoons of the soy sauce, ¼ cup of the rice wine, the seasoned rice vinegar, sugar, hot chili oil, minced scallion, ginger, and half of the garlic. Divide among six small bowls and set aside.

2. Place the meat in a medium bowl. Make a marinade from the remaining 2 tablespoons soy sauce, 1 tablespoon rice wine, sesame oil, and hot pepper. Pour over the beef; toss lightly. Arrange the meat attractively on a large platter along with the shrimp, tofu, mushrooms, scallion pieces, carrots, and greens.

3. In a wok or wide saucepan, heat the peanut oil. Add the remaining garlic and stir-fry 30 seconds. Add the Chinese cabbage and the remaining 2 tablespoons rice wine and stir-fry until the cabbage wilts, 1½ to 2 minutes. Add the chicken stock, salt, and a pinch of hot pepper, if desired. Bring to a boil, reduce the heat to low, and simmer 20 minutes.

4. To serve, add small amounts of the mushrooms, scallion pieces, carrots, and greens to the boiling stock. Cook until tender, letting diners help themselves to these ingredients as they are cooked. At the same time, diners can use chopsticks to dip beef and shrimp into the broth, keeping it immersed until cooked, and then dip the items into the sauce.

To make commercial **chili oil**, hot red chili peppers are steeped in vegetable or sesame oil to release their heat and flavor. The result is a red, fragrant, spicy seasoning that is a mainstay of Chinese cooking. You can purchase chili oil from Asian markets or well-stocked food stores, and it will keep six months at room temperature or longer if refrigerated.

Fresh **ginger**, also called gingerroot, isn't a root at all. It's actually the knobby underground stem, or *rhizome*, of the ginger plant. (Other rhizomes include turmeric and galangal.) A powerful and versatile seasoning, ginger can cross over from savory to sweet dishes. Select fresh ginger with a plump, smooth, and slightly shiny skin. If it's wrinkled or cracked, the ginger is drying and past its prime. To prepare fresh ginger, first use a vegetable peeler or sharp knife to remove the thin skin. Then, depending upon your recipe, slice, dice, mince, grate, shred, or juice it just like garlic. If pressed, you can always substitute the minced or puréed ginger that's available in jars.

Onion Soup Olé

This far-reaching variation on the classic French onion soup is abundantly flavored with onions and some unexpected chili peppers and spices playing in the background. Using canned broth is not recommended for this recipe.

MAKES:
4 to 6 servings
PREP:
10 minutes
COOK:
55 minutes

3	tablespoons unsalted butter
1	teaspoon cumin seeds
3	large yellow onions (about 2 pounds total), thinly sliced
1	pasilla or other dried chili pepper
	Stems from 1 bunch of cilantro, tied into a bundle with heavy string
	Salt
1	tablespoon flour
6	cups beef stock
4 to 6	slices slightly stale Italian bread
½	of a poblano or green bell pepper, seeded and finely diced
4 to 6	thick slices Monterey Jack cheese (about 1 ounce each)

1 In a large heavy saucepan, melt the butter with the cumin seeds over medium heat. Add the onions, pasilla pepper, cilantro stems, and about ¼ teaspoon salt. Place a piece of wax paper directly on top of the onions and cook until they begin to give off some of their own liquid, 3 to 4 minutes. Remove the paper and cook, stirring often, until the onions are a tawny brown, 35 to 40 minutes. (This is a slow process that mustn't be hurried by too much heat. The onions must not scorch. Toward the end of cooking, watch closely.)

2 Sprinkle the flour over the onions, stir in, and cook 1 minute. Add the beef stock and bring to a boil. Taste and see if the chili pepper has added the right amount of heat. Remove it if so; otherwise, leave it in. Cover partially and simmer for 10 minutes. Remove and discard the cilantro and chili.

3 Preheat the broiler. Place the bread slices on a large cookie sheet and broil 4 to 6 inches from the heat source until lightly toasted, 1 to 2 minutes per side. Place one bread slice in each of four to six heatproof soup crocks. Ladle the soup over and add a sprinkle of diced poblano peppers. Top with a slice of cheese and broil briefly, just until the cheese melts and bubbles at the edges, 1 to 2 minutes, watching carefully. Serve at once.

Vegetable Gumbo

Based on a traditional roux and spiced with a generous hand, this gumbo has all the familiar trappings of the classic versions that help to define New Orleans cooking—everything except meat, that is. Instead, a collection of colorful vegetables lies at the heat of it, imbuing the gumbo with a fresh, lively taste.

MAKES:
4 to 6 servings
PREP:
30 minutes
COOK:
20 minutes

1 In a large, heavy saucepan, heat the oil over medium-high heat. When it is almost smoking, whisk in the flour. Cook, stirring constantly, until the mixture turns a rich brown color, 3 to 5 minutes. As soon as the desired color is reached, carefully add the onion, leek, celery, and bell peppers; use caution because the hot oil will splatter. Cook, stirring often, for 3 minutes. Add the garlic and seasoning blend and cook 1 minute longer.

2 Add the stock, okra, squash, corn, tomatoes, and salt. Reduce the heat to medium and cook gently until the okra is crisp-tender, about 10 minutes. Season with hot sauce to taste before serving.

¼   cup vegetable oil or rendered duck fat
¼   cup flour

1   medium onion, finely diced
1   leek, finely diced
2   celery ribs, finely diced
1   small red bell pepper, finely diced
1   small green bell pepper, finely diced

1   large garlic clove, minced
2   tablespoons Cajun seasoning blend

6   cups vegetable stock or canned broth
⅓   pound okra, cut into ½-inch-thick slices
1   chayote squash or medium zucchini, cut into ½-inch dice
1   cup corn kernels, preferably white
3   plum tomatoes, diced
¼   teaspoon salt

Hot red pepper sauce

With the right recipe collection, dinner can be made, start to finish, in less than an hour, and it's just this kind of speed that cooks clamor for. Although weekday dinners most often demand careful economy of time, weekends also can find schedules filled a little too tightly to allow for leisurely hours spent in the kitchen on meal preparation.

Speedy dinners—those that can be put together and cooked in short order—are a welcome and necessary part of your repertoire. All the better if they're also made in one pot for added ease of cooking and cleanup. Fragrant stir-fries, such as the **Stir-Fry of Beef, Asparagus & Bell Peppers**, with exotic Asian undertones and modern ease; simple sautés, such as **Vietnamese Basil Chicken with Peppers**, that combine a world of influences; and quick, robust ragouts, like the **Sausages with Potatoes & Peppers**, can all come to the table on short notice.

Speedy Dinners

Skillets and woks are key pieces of equipment for the speediest of speedy cooking. A large, sturdy skillet is invaluable, with countless uses. For one-pot cooking, a good quality 12-inch skillet allows maximum flexibility. Its generous size allows foods to be cooked evenly and efficiently without overcrowding. The goal of reducing fat leads many cooks to choose a nonstick skillet. Enormously improved over the earliest models, nonstick finishes are now much stronger and scratch-resistant.

Woks are enjoying a renewed interest that takes them beyond the realm of Asian cooking. They can be called on to double as a skillet, masterfully handling almost any type of sautéed meal. Carbon steel woks are most common and traditional, but other, heavier ones are also available. Enamel-coated and anodized aluminum woks are sturdier and more durable, which makes them perfectly suited to contemporary cooking styles.

Sausages with Potatoes & Peppers

Although markets once offered little more in sausages than Italian and Polish, a much wider variety is now available. It's as likely you'll find smoked duck sausage with brandy, Thai chicken, andouille, and Santa Fe turkey sausage keeping company with the more familiar types. Use a fanciful mix of several kinds in this hearty mélange and be sure to have lots of bread on hand.

MAKES:
4 servings

PREP:
15 minutes

COOK:
25 minutes

1 In a large skillet, heat the olive oil over medium-high heat. Add the sausage and cook, turning, until nicely browned, 5 to 7 minutes. Pour off all but 1 tablespoon of the fat.

2 Add the onion, bell peppers, and potatoes and mix well. Pour in the wine, then the marinara sauce, basil, and hot red pepper.

3 Cover and simmer over medium-low heat until the potatoes are tender, about 20 minutes.

1	**tablespoon olive oil**
1¼	**pounds sausage in casing, preferably a mix of several types, cut into 2-inch pieces**
1	**large onion, cut into thin wedges**
1	**small red bell pepper, cut into 1-inch strips**
1	**small green bell pepper, cut into 1-inch strips**
4	**small red potatoes, quartered lengthwise**
½	**cup dry red wine**
½	**cup marinara or tomato sauce**
½	**teaspoon dried basil**
	Pinch of crushed hot red pepper

El Paso Potato & Chorizo Hash with Poached Eggs

Hash is one those universal dishes that seems appropriate for any meal. It happens to be one of my favorite choices for brunch. Here, leftover cooked potatoes are put to great use: crisply fried together with an irresistible mix of Tex-Mex flavors. If you don't have any leftover cooked potatoes in your fridge, boil up a few the night before or zap them in the microwave until just tender.

MAKES:
4 servings

PREP:
15 minutes

COOK:
25 minutes

4   **eggs**

¼   **pound Mexican-style chorizo or hot Italian sausage**

¼   **cup vegetable oil**

1   **medium onion, cut into ½-inch dice**

1   **pound leftover cooked potatoes, peeled and cut into ½-inch dice**

1   **small bell pepper (red, yellow, or green), cut into ½-inch dice**

1   **fresh jalapeño or serrano pepper, seeded and minced**

¼   **teaspoon ground cumin**

¼   **teaspoon salt**

⅛ to ¼   **teaspoon cayenne, to taste**

½   **cup chopped cilantro**

Tomato salsa
Warm flour or corn tortillas

1 To poach eggs, fill a large skillet about half full with water and bring to a boil. Reduce the heat so the water is simmering. Crack each egg into a small cup and carefully slip into the water. Simmer until the eggs are cooked as desired, 4 to 6 minutes for a firm white and soft center. Carefully remove the eggs with a slotted spoon and set aside in a warm spot. Wipe out the skillet.

2 Crumble the sausage into the skillet. Cook over medium heat, stirring to break up any clumps of meat, until the sausage is lightly browned, about 5 minutes. With a slotted spoon, transfer the sausage to paper towels to drain. Drain the fat from the skillet.

3 Heat the oil in the same skillet. Add the onion, potatoes, bell pepper, and jalapeño. Season with the cumin, salt, and cayenne. Cook over medium–high heat 5 minutes. Reduce the heat to medium and continue to cook, stirring occasionally, until the potatoes and onions are well browned, about 10 minutes longer.

4 Stir in the chorizo and cilantro and remove from the heat. To serve, top each portion with a poached egg. Pass salsa and warm tortillas on the side.

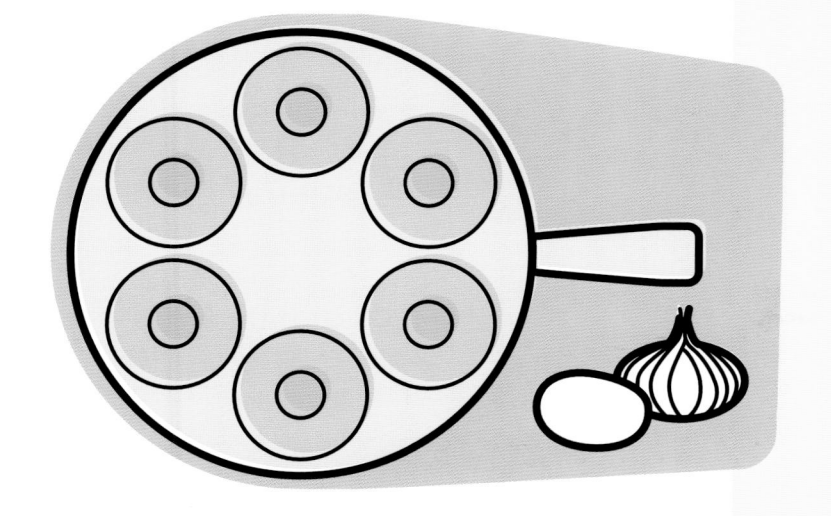

Highly seasoned with chili powder, garlic, and other spices, **chorizo** is a coarsely ground pork sausage. Made with fresh pork, the Mexican version of chorizo requires cooking. Spanish chorizo is created from dry-cured smoked pork and does not require cooking. Available in larger grocery stores and Latin supermarkets, chorizo can be a tasty ingredient in many dishes, such as casseroles, soups, stews, and enchiladas.

In Chinese, **cilantro** means "fragrant plant." Also called Chinese parsley, Vietnamese parsley, or fresh coriander, this herb is simply the bright green leaves and stems of the coriander plant. It resembles feathery, flat-leaf parsley, and its sharp, aromatic, somewhat astringent flavor adds zip to many dishes. Cilantro tastes like a unique blend of sage and citrus; its sharp, earthy freshness delivers a gentle bite. Commonly used in Asian, Caribbean, and Latin American cooking, cilantro's distinctive flavor acts as a counterpoint to highly spiced foods. You'll find cilantro sold in bunches year-round in most supermarkets. Choose leaves of a bright, even color with no sign of wilting.

Santa Fe Chicken
with Black Beans, Corn & Poblanos

From the bold colors to the fresh taste, there's a lot about this simple sauté that suggests summer. But the vegetables used here are available all year, making summery meals possible anytime. For extra dazzle and crunchy contrast, fry slivers of corn tortillas until they are crisp and serve the chicken atop them.

MAKES:
4 servings

PREP:
20 minutes

COOK:
15 minutes

1½   **tablespoons vegetable oil**

4   **skinless, boneless chicken breast halves, cut into 1- to 1½-inch pieces**

½   **teaspoon chili powder**

½   **teaspoon ground coriander**

½   **teaspoon salt**

1   **medium zucchini, diced**

¾   **cup corn kernels**

1   **small roasted poblano pepper (see Note), finely diced**

½   **cup chicken broth**

½   **cup heavy cream**

¾   **cup canned black beans**

2   **teaspoons fresh lime juice**

2   **tablespoons chopped cilantro**

3   **scallions, thinly sliced**

4   **lime wedges**

1 In a large nonstick skillet, heat 1 tablespoon of the oil over high heat. Add the chicken, and season with the chili powder, coriander, and ¼ teaspoon of the salt. Cook and stir until the chicken is lightly browned at the edges, 3 to 4 minutes. Remove the chicken from the skillet, and set aside.

2 Heat the remaining ½ tablespoon oil in the same pan. Add the zucchini, corn, poblano pepper, and the remaining ¼ teaspoon salt. Cook until the vegetables begin to brown at the edges, 4 to 5 minutes.

3 Add the chicken stock and boil for 1 to 2 minutes. Add the cream, beans, chicken, and lime juice. Reduce the heat to medium and cook until the chicken is no longer pink in the center and the sauce has thickened slightly, 3 to 4 minutes. Remove the pan from the heat and stir in the scallions. Sprinkle cilantro on top and serve with lime wedges.

To **roast peppers**, arrange them on a baking sheet and broil 8 inches from the heat source until they are blackened all over, turning them as necessary. Alternately, they can be roasted by charring them directly over a gas flame, turning them with tongs so they blacken evenly. Transfer the roasted peppers to a paper bag, seal tightly, and let stand 10 minutes to loosen the skin. Slip off the blackened skin and remove the core and seeds.

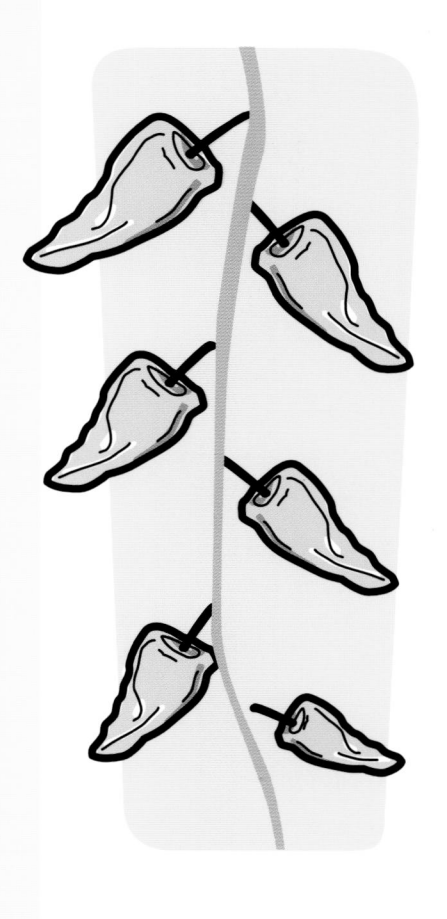

The **poblano** is a mild to medium-hot pepper that averages 4 inches in length. Dark green, maturing to red or brown, the poblano is heart-shaped, wide at the top, tapering to a blunt point. It holds up well to grilling, which enhances its rich, fruity-smoky taste. There are three different names for this pepper: *poblano* when it is fresh, and *ancho* and *mulato* when dried. Suitable substitutes for the poblano would be the Anaheim pepper, bell pepper, or the hotter serrano pepper.

Stir-Fry of Beef, Asparagus & Bell Peppers

Briskly stirring small pieces of food over very high heat in a wok or skillet is a well-regarded, low-fat cooking technique. Stir-frying ensures that vegetables, such as the fresh asparagus and bell pepper used here, remain crisp and nutritious.

MAKES:
4 servings

PREP:
15 minutes

MARINADE:
2 to 12 hours

COOK:
20 minutes

3 tablespoons reduced-sodium soy sauce

2 tablespoons hoisin sauce

2 tablespoons seasoned rice vinegar

4 teaspoons Asian sesame oil

4 teaspoons honey

4 teaspoons brown sugar

1 large garlic clove, minced

2 teaspoons minced fresh ginger

1 teaspoon Asian chili paste

1¼ pounds beef sirloin, cut into thin strips

1 (3½- to 4-ounce) package bean thread or cellophane noodles

3 tablespoons peanut oil

¼ teaspoon salt

1 pound slender asparagus, cut into 1-inch pieces

1 large red bell pepper, diced

3 scallions, 2 minced and 1 thinly sliced

1 In a small bowl, combine the soy sauce, hoisin sauce, vinegar, sesame oil, honey, brown sugar, garlic, ginger, and ½ teaspoon of the chili paste. Transfer half of the soy sauce mixture to a large plastic food storage bag. Add the meat to the bag, seal tightly, and refrigerate 2 to 12 hours.

2 Place the noodles in a large heatproof bowl and cover with hot water. Let stand 15 to 20 minutes, until softened. Drain well and squeeze out as much moisture as possible. Return the noodles to the bowl and toss with 1 tablespoon of the peanut oil and the remaining ½ teaspoon chili paste. Season with the salt.

3 In a wok or large skillet, heat 1 tablespoon peanut oil over high heat. Add the asparagus and bell pepper and stir-fry until the vegetables begin to brown at the edges, 3 to 4 minutes. Remove the vegetables from the wok and set aside.

4 Heat the remaining 1 tablespoon peanut oil in the wok. Add the minced scallions and stir-fry 30 seconds. Add the meat and stir-fry until no longer pink, 1 to 2 minutes. Add the cooked vegetables, sliced scallion, and reserved soy sauce mixture and cook just until heated through, 30 to 40 seconds. Serve at once.

Puebla-Style Burritos

Just about every cuisine has an ingenious method of tucking food into its own edible wrapper. Here, soft flour tortillas encase a deep red, chili-flavored mix of meat and cheese.

MAKES:
8 burritos

PREP:
15 minutes

COOK:
30 minutes

1 Rinse the chili peppers and place in a small heatproof bowl. Cover with boiling water and let stand 15 minutes. Remove the stems and seeds.

2 In a heavy skillet (do not use a skillet with a nonstick finish), cook the tomatoes and jalapeño pepper over high heat, turning occasionally, until the skin on the tomatoes is charred, 7 to 9 minutes. Core the tomatoes and seed the pepper.

3 Transfer the tomatoes, jalapeño pepper, and chili peppers to a blender and puree until smooth. Set aside.

4 Heat the oil in the same skillet over high heat. Add the onions, ¼ teaspoon of the salt, and the oregano. Cook, stirring often, until the onions begin to brown, about 5 minutes. Add the vinegar and brown sugar. Reduce the heat to medium and cook, stirring occasionally, until the onions are soft, 4 to 5 minutes.

5 Add the chicken, chicken stock, tomato mixture, and remaining ¼ teaspoon salt, and simmer until heated through, 3 to 4 minutes. To serve, spoon into warm tortillas and sprinkle with desired amounts of the cilantro and cheese.

---

2   guajillo or ancho chili peppers

4   small plum tomatoes
1   jalapeño pepper

1   tablespoon vegetable oil
2   medium onions, cut into ¼-inch wedges
½   teaspoon salt, or to taste
¼   teaspoon dried oregano leaves

2½ tablespoons cider vinegar
1   tablespoon brown sugar

4   cups shredded cooked chicken or beef
½   cup chicken stock or reduced-sodium canned broth

8   flour tortillas, warmed
    Cilantro, minced
    Crumbled queso fresco or shredded Monterey Jack cheese

Vietnamese Basil Chicken with Peppers

MAKES:
3 to 4 servings

PREP:
10 minutes

MARINADE:
30 minutes to 5 hours

SOAK:
30 minutes

COOK:
10 minutes

Simple, lively, and slightly exotic, this colorful dish indulges in a cross-cultural pairing of Vietnamese and Thai tastes.

¼ cup oyster sauce

1 tablespoon honey

1 tablespoon hoisin sauce

1 tablespoon fish sauce (nam pla) or soy sauce

1 large egg yolk

2 to 3 teaspoons Asian chili paste

2 stalks of lemongrass, trimmed and minced as finely as possible

4 skinless, boneless chicken breast halves

6 to 8 ounces Thai rice noodles

⅓ cup chicken stock or reduced-sodium canned broth

¼ teaspoon salt

2 tablespoons peanut or other vegetable oil

1 large red bell pepper, cut into ½-inch squares

4 scallions, sliced

¼ cup minced fresh basil

3 tablespoons finely minced cashews

1 In a medium bowl, combine the oyster sauce, honey, hoisin sauce, fish sauce, egg yolk, 1 teaspoon of the chili paste, and the lemongrass. Mix well. Add the chicken and toss. Transfer to a large plastic food storage bag, seal tightly, and refrigerate 30 minutes or up to 5 hours. Place the noodles in a large bowl and cover with hot water. Let stand for 30 minutes, until soft; drain well.

2 In a large skillet or wok, heat the chicken stock, salt, and remaining chili paste to a simmer. Add the noodles, mix well, and cook just until hot, about 1 minute. Transfer the noodles to a serving platter and cover to keep warm.

3 In the same pan, heat the peanut oil over high heat. Add the bell pepper squares and cook, stirring often, until they begin to soften, 2 to 3 minutes. Add the chicken and marinade and stir-fry just until the chicken is cooked through, 3 to 4 minutes. Stir in the scallions and basil and remove from the heat. Spoon over the noodles and sprinkle with the cashews.

Scallops with Corn, Bacon & Tomatoes

Summer is practically written into this gloriously easy and luxurious recipe. It's an ideal dish to make during those happy but regrettably short weeks when sweet corn, tomatoes, and leeks all take their place at the farmers' market.

MAKES:
3 to 4 servings
PREP:
15 minutes
COOK:
10 minutes

1 Cook the bacon in a large nonstick skillet, over medium heat, turning, until it is lightly browned, about 5 minutes. Add the leeks and cook over high heat until they begin to soften, 1 to 2 minutes.

2 Add the scallops and reduce the heat slightly. Cook, shaking the pan often, until they are opaque in the center, about 2 minutes.

3 Add the corn, tomato, and cream, and bring to a boil. Remove the pan from the heat. Stir in the basil, thyme, salt, and cayenne. Serve at once.

2　strips of thick-sliced bacon, cut into ¼-inch dice

1　medium leek (white and tender green), cut into ½-inch dice

1　pound scallops, preferably small sea scallops, rinsed and patted dry

1　cup corn kernels, preferably fresh

1　large tomato, seeded and cut into ½-inch dice

3　tablespoons heavy cream

2　tablespoons minced fresh basil

2　teaspoons minced fresh thyme

¼　teaspoon salt, or more to taste

Pinch of cayenne

Lebanese Chicken with Bulgur Salad

Bulgur is often overlooked in the endless quest for easy-to-prepare foods. It requires no cooking, just simple soaking in hot water. Here, the bulgur, dressed with lots of garden herbs and subtle flavors, comes to the table with mildly spiced, seared chicken breasts. The proportions of water and bulgur in this recipe give slightly chewy results. If you prefer a more tender grain, add several more tablespoons of water.

MAKES:
4 servings

PREP:
10 minutes

SOAK:
20 minutes

COOK:
15 minutes

1	cup bulgur
1	tablespoon tomato paste

1	tablespoon ground cumin
1½	teaspoons hot paprika
¾	teaspoon ground coriander

¾	teaspoon salt, or to taste
3	tablespoons orange juice
3	tablespoons olive oil

4	skinless, boneless chicken breast halves

1	small onion, finely diced
1	medium tomato, diced
¾	cup minced mixed fresh herbs such as mint, dill, cilantro, and parsley

1 In a large heatproof bowl, combine the bulgur with 1 cup hot water and the tomato paste. Stir to mix well. Cover tightly and let stand until the water is absorbed, about 20 minutes.

2 In a large cast-iron griddle or skillet, combine the cumin, paprika, and coriander. Place over high heat and cook, stirring occasionally, until the spices are fragrant, 30 to 60 seconds. Transfer the spices to a small dish and add the salt, orange juice, and 1½ tablespoons of the olive oil. Add 1 tablespoon of this spice mixture to the bulgur, and use the rest to rub onto both sides of the chicken.

3 Add the onion, tomato, mixed fresh herbs, and remaining 1½ tablespoons olive oil to the bulgur mixture. Season with additional salt to taste.

4 Heat the griddle or skillet over high heat. When it is very hot, add the chicken. Cook, turning once, until the chicken is no longer pink in the center, 8 to 9 minutes. Serve the chicken atop the bulgur mixture.

Bulgur has a delicious nutty taste and a tender, chewy texture. This makes it a very popular and nutritious staple in the Middle East, where it's used in many dishes, most notably tabouli and pilaf. To produce bulgur and speed up its cooking time, whole wheat kernels are washed, dried, and crushed into coarse, medium, or fine particles. You can buy bulgur prepackaged or in bulk at grocery stores and health-food markets.

A good sharp knife and a wooden chopping board are your best tools for mincing most **fresh herbs.** Use a 7-inch blade that is slightly curved or a double-handled *mezzaluna*. (In Italian, mezzaluna means "half moon," implying the shape of this utensil's arched blade.) Some herbs, such a fresh chives, are better minced with kitchen scissors.

Mincing Herbs with a Chef's Knife

1. Remove the stems of the herbs, if needed, and pile the leaves on the cutting board.
2. Hold the top of the knife tip on the board with your fingers. Use a rocking motion to mince the herbs, keeping them in a pile as you chop them into very fine pieces.

Mincing Herbs with a Mezzaluna

1. Strip the leaves from the stems if needed, and then spread out the herbs on the chopping board.
2. Hold the mezzaluna firmly by its knobs. With a rolling motion, seesaw the blades over the fresh herbs, chopping them as roughly or as finely as you desire.

Chopping Herbs with Scissors

1. Remove the leaves from the stems as needed, discard the stems, and then place the leaves in a measuring cup or small bowl.
2. Use sharp kitchen scissors to snip the herbs into small pieces.

Coco Beach Citrus Chicken Stir-Fry

*There may never be enough recipes for chicken, especially for boneless breasts.
They're economical, cook quickly, and are endlessly versatile. All those traits are deliciously
exploited in this colorful sauté that is perhaps best described as "fusion food"
—a mix of new American techniques and bright Latin flavors.*

MAKES:
4 servings

PREP:
25 minutes

COOK:
12 minutes

2   tablespoons unsalted butter

1   large red bell pepper, cut into
2 x ½-inch strips

1   medium onion, cut into thin wedges

1   large garlic clove, minced

¼   cup finely diced smoked ham

1   teaspoon grated orange zest

½   teaspoon grated lime zest

½   teaspoon salt, or to taste

Pinch of cayenne

1¼   pounds skinless, boneless chicken breasts,
cut into ¾-inch strips

Juice of 1 medium orange

Juice of 1 medium lime

2   tablespoons cognac or brandy

1   teaspoon honey

1   small serrano or jalapeño pepper, seeded
and minced

¼   cup canned unsweetened coconut milk

3   scallions, thinly sliced

1   small head of romaine lettuce, shredded
(about 4 cups)

1 In a large skillet, melt 1 tablespoon of the butter over medium-high heat. Add the bell pepper, onion, garlic, ham, orange zest, lime zest, ¼ teaspoon of the salt, and the cayenne. Cook, stirring often, until the onion and bell pepper are crisp-tender, 4 to 5 minutes. Remove the vegetable mixture from the pan and set aside.

2 Melt the remaining 1 tablespoon butter in the same pan. Add the chicken and the remaining ¼ teaspoon salt. Cook over medium-high heat, stirring often, until the chicken is no longer pink in the center, 3 to 4 minutes. Set aside with the vegetable mixture.

3 Add the orange juice, lime juice, brandy, honey, and hot pepper to the skillet. Boil 1 minute. Return the chicken and vegetables to the skillet. Add the coconut milk and scallions. Cook just until heated through, 2 to 3 minutes. Serve on a bed of shredded lettuce.

The aromatic oils in **citrus zest** add a lot of flavor to foods. Only the colored part of the skin, its fragrant outermost skin layer, and not its bitter white pith, is considered the zest. You can remove it with a vegetable peeler, paring knife, or citrus zester. The sharp cutting edge of a citrus zester has five small holes that create threadlike strips of peel when pulled across the surface of fruit.

You can easily **strip chicken skin** by hand, with the occasional assistance of a knife or kitchen scissors to release the skin from the meat. Place a half breast, skin-side up, on the cutting board. Holding the piece with one hand, pull the skin away from the meat with the other hand, starting at the narrow end. Use the same technique for skinning chicken thighs.

Named after Jalapa, the capital of Veracruz, Mexico, **jalapeño chili peppers** range from hot to very hot. Smooth and dark green, or scarlet when ripe, they have a rounded tip and measure about 2 inches long and 1 inch in diameter. Besides their flavor, jalapeños enjoy popularity because they're so easily seeded—the seeds and veins are extremely hot. They're available fresh and canned; in their dried form, jalapeños are known as chipotles.

Soft-Shell Crab Tostadas

Soft-shell crabs are a rare treasure to be sure, a seasonal indulgence that deserves to be explored at every chance. Many cooks will say that the best way to cook them is the simplest: pan frying in seasoned flour. There's an abundance of truth in that tradition, but it doesn't mean that they can't be garnished in a completely delicious and unexpected way.

MAKES:
4 servings

PREP:
10 minutes

COOK:
25 minutes

1   cup cooked or canned black beans

½   cup chopped red bell pepper

½   cup chopped poblano pepper

1   small onion, chopped

1   tablespoon vegetable oil

1   tablespoon cider vinegar

1   bunch of cilantro, leaves only

1   teaspoon ground cumin

¾   teaspoon salt

   Cayenne

1   cup sour cream

8   soft-shell crabs, cleaned

⅔   cup flour

3   tablespoons yellow cornmeal

Vegetable oil, for frying

4   corn tortillas

½   cup tomato salsa

½   cup guacamole

1   lime, cut into wedges

1 Make a black bean salsa by combining the beans, bell pepper, poblano pepper, onion, oil, vinegar, 2 tablespoons of the cilantro leaves, the cumin, ¼ teaspoon of the salt, and a pinch of cayenne in a food processor. Pulse on and off until the mixture is uniformly chopped but not pureed. Set the black bean salsa aside.

2 For the cilantro cream, put the remaining cilantro leaves in a strainer and immerse in boiling water 5 seconds. Drain well and pat dry. Puree in a food processor with the sour cream and a pinch each of salt and cayenne until smooth.

3 At cooking time, pat the crabs dry. In a large plastic food storage bag, combine the flour, cornmeal, remaining ½ teaspoon salt, and a pinch of cayenne. Add 1 crab at a time and shake gently to coat with the flour mixture.

4 In a large skillet, heat ½ inch of oil. Add the tortillas and cook briefly, just until they begin to crisp, about 30 seconds. Drain on paper towels.

5 Add the crabs to the hot oil in batches without crowding. Cook, turning once, until crisp and golden on both sides, about 5 minutes per batch.

6 To serve, spoon the black bean salsa over the tortillas. Arrange 2 crabs atop each and spoon the salsa, guacamole, and cilantro cream around the edge. Garnish with lime wedges.

During their life cycles, blue crabs shed their shells to grow larger ones. Soon afterward, their skins harden into new shells. During those few days before the new shells harden, we refer to these crustaceans as **soft-shell crabs**. Always sold whole, they are in season from April to mid-September, with a peak in June and July.

To clean a soft shell crab, use a paring knife or kitchen scissors to cut away three distinct parts: the lungs, the apron, and the head. The lungs are right under each side of the pointed end of the top shell, and the apron is at the opposite end of the crab from the head.

Pad Thai

One of the most popular Thai noodle dishes is easily made at home, with results closely mimicking the best renditions. It's a very adaptable dish as well as a great vehicle for leftover bits of meat or poultry, from Chinese barbecued pork to shreds of chicken or even tofu. Like all stir-fried dishes, this one goes very quickly once it's on the stove, so make sure all the ingredients are assembled as described.

MAKES:
2 to 3 servings
PREP:
15 minutes
STAND:
30 minutes
COOK:
10 minutes

5 to 6	ounces Thai rice noodles	

3 tablespoons Thai fish sauce (nam pla) or soy sauce

1½ tablespoons sugar

1 tablespoon ketchup

¼ to ½ teaspoon chili paste

4 scallions, 2 minced and 2 cut into slivers

2 large eggs, lightly beaten

½ cup minced cilantro, plus additional sprigs for garnish

¼ cup roasted unsalted peanuts

Pinch of crushed hot red pepper

3 tablespoons vegetable oil

½ cup finely julienned carrots

4 ounces small peeled shrimp

2 large garlic cloves, minced

¾ cup bean sprouts or snow pea sprouts

Mint leaves

Lime wedges

1 Place the noodles in a medium bowl and cover with hot water. Let stand until they are softened, about 30 minutes. Drain well and let stand for 10 to 15 minutes.

2 In a small bowl, combine the fish sauce, sugar, ketchup, and chili paste. Mix well. In a medium bowl, add half of the minced scallions to the beaten eggs along with 2 tablespoons of the minced cilantro.

3 On a cutting board, combine the remaining minced scallions and minced cilantro with the peanuts and crushed hot pepper. Mince together and set aside.

4 In a wok or large skillet, heat the oil over high heat. Add the carrots and scallions and stir-fry 20 seconds. Add the shrimp and garlic and stir-fry just until the shrimp begins to turn white, about 1½ minutes. Add the fish sauce mixture, taking care to add all the sugar that may have settled at the bottom of the dish. Stir well and cook 30 seconds.

5 Add the eggs and cook until they begin to scramble, about 1 minute. Add the noodles and about ¼ cup of the sprouts, tossing so they are well coated with the egg mixture. Cook until the noodles are hot, about 1 minute.

6 Transfer the noodle mixture to a serving platter and sprinkle the peanut mixture on top. Arrange the remaining sprouts, cilantro sprigs, and mint leaves in a cluster at one end of the platter and garnish with lime wedges.

Made from rice flour and water, **rice noodles** come in a variety of shapes and sizes, from fine, brittle vermicelli to broader noodles. Shoppers will probably find the greatest choice in Asian groceries. In addition to soaking the noodles and stir-frying them, you also can fry rice noodles and add them to soups.

Fish sauce, also referred to as fish gravy, is a mixture based on the liquid from salted, fermented fish, usually anchovies. Popular throughout Southeast Asia, this thin liquid ranges in color from ochre to deep brown. Fish sauces may be variously flavored with chili peppers or sugar, depending upon the intended use. Asian markets carry a wide variety of these extremely pungent sauces, including *nam pla* (Thai), *nuoc nam* (Vietnamese), *patis* (Philippines), and *shottsuru* (Japanese). Use fish sauce as a condiment and flavoring or as a seasoning while cooking dishes.

Widely used in Asian cooking, **chili paste** is a blend of hot chili peppers, garlic, oil, and salt. As an ingredient or a condiment, chili paste adds a rich, fiery flavor to many dishes. *Nam prik pao* is the Thai version of chili paste. It's made of chilies, onions, sugar, shrimp paste, fish sauce, and sometimes tamarind. You can purchase chili paste from Asian grocery stores and many large supermarkets.

Bourbon-Glazed Ham Steaks with Snap Pea Succotash

MAKES:
3 to 4 servings

PREP:
15 minutes

MARINADE:
30 minutes or overnight

COOK:
20 minutes

Tender, sweet snap peas replace lima beans in the traditional succotash.

¼ cup bourbon

1 tablespoon pure maple syrup

¾ teaspoon grainy Dijon or honey mustard

1 pound ham steaks

2½ tablespoons unsalted butter

1 small sweet onion, finely diced

2 small celery ribs, finely diced

1 small red bell pepper, finely diced

¼ pound small sugar snap peas, trimmed

1 cup corn kernels

½ cup ham stock, chicken stock, or reduced-sodium canned chicken broth

½ teaspoon dried thyme leaves

½ teaspoon coarsely cracked black pepper

¼ teaspoon salt, or to taste

1 large tomato, seeded and diced

2 scallions, sliced

1 tablespoon minced fresh chives

1 In a large plastic food storage bag, combine 3½ tablespoons bourbon, the maple syrup, and ½ teaspoon mustard. Add the ham, seal the bag tightly, and let stand for at least 30 minutes or refrigerate overnight.

2 Remove the ham from the plastic bag, reserving the marinade. In a large, heavy skillet, melt 1 tablespoon of the butter over high heat. When it is bubbly, add the ham. Cook, turning several times, until the ham begins to brown, about 5 minutes. Add the reserved marinade and continue to cook until the ham is nicely glazed, 5 minutes. Transfer the ham to a heated platter, cover, and set aside.

3 Melt the remaining 1½ tablespoons butter in the same pan over medium-high heat. Add the onion and celery and cook until they begin to soften, 3 to 4 minutes. Add the bell pepper, snap peas, corn, ham stock, thyme, black pepper, salt, and the remaining ¼ teaspoon mustard. Bring to a boil and cook until the peas are tender, 3 to 4 minutes. Add the remaining 1½ teaspoons bourbon, the tomato, and the scallions and remove from the heat. Spoon over the ham and sprinkle with the chives.

Summer Chicken & Vegetable Sauté

Dazzling colors and the savory aroma of a flourishing herb garden make this a perfect summer dish. Once all the ingredients are sliced and assembled, the cooking is quick. A wok works best since its generous size allows the food to cook evenly without overcrowding.

MAKES:
4 servings

PREP:
20 minutes

COOK:
10 minutes

1 In a wok, heat 2 tablespoons of the olive oil over high heat. Add the chicken and season lightly with salt and pepper. Cook and stir just until the chicken is no longer pink, 2 to 3 minutes. Remove from the wok and set aside.

2 Heat the remaining 2 tablespoons oil over high heat. Add the bell peppers, zucchini, sugar snap peas, and salt and pepper to taste. Stir-fry just until they are crisp-tender, 2 to 3 minutes. Set aside with the chicken.

3 Add the Marsala, tomatoes, thyme, and tarragon to the wok. Boil until the liquid is almost cooked away, about 3 minutes. Return the chicken and vegetables to the wok and stir lightly. Cook 1 minute, just to heat through. Add the vinegar or lemon juice and basil, season with salt and pepper to taste, and serve at once.

¼ **cup olive oil**

4 **skinless, boneless chicken breast halves, cut into 1½-inch pieces**

Salt and freshly ground pepper

1 **large red bell pepper, cut into 1-inch squares**

1 **large yellow bell pepper, cut into 1-inch squares**

2 **small zucchini, sliced ¼ inch thick**

¼ **pound sugar snap peas**

¼ **cup Marsala wine**

2 **large tomatoes, seeded and chopped**

1 **tablespoon minced fresh thyme leaves or ½ teaspoon dried**

1 **tablespoon minced fresh tarragon leaves or ½ teaspoon dried**

1 **tablespoon seasoned rice vinegar or lemon juice**

1 **tablespoon minced fresh basil**

Transparent Noodles with Stir-Fried Turkey & Asparagus

More stylized in its presentation than most Asian stir-fries, this one comes to the table with three separate layers. A wreath of colorful vegetables and a center of ground turkey sit atop a big cushion of noodles.

MAKES:
4 servings

PREP:
10 minutes

STAND:
15 to 20 minutes

COOK:
5 minutes

1   (3½- to 4-ounce) package bean threads or cellophane noodles

1   pound ground turkey
1   tablespoon dry sherry
1   tablespoon seasoned rice vinegar
1   tablespoon cornstarch
2   teaspoons soy sauce
½ to 1   teaspoon red chili paste

1   cup bean sprouts

1   tablespoon plus 1 teaspoon peanut or other vegetable oil
2   teaspoons Asian sesame oil
    Salt
2   teaspoons minced fresh ginger
1   scallion, minced

½   pound pencil-thin asparagus, diagonally cut into ¾-inch pieces
½   of a medium red bell pepper, chopped

1 Place the bean threads in a large bowl and cover with hot water. Let stand until softened, 15 to 20 minutes. Meanwhile, in a medium bowl, combine the turkey, sherry, vinegar, cornstarch, soy sauce, and chili paste. Mix lightly with your hands until well blended.

2 Drain the bean threads and squeeze them gently to remove excess water. Use scissors to randomly snip them into shorter lengths. (It's okay if they're not uniform.) Toss the bean threads with the bean sprouts and transfer to a large serving platter.

3 In a large skillet or wok, heat 1 teaspoon each of the peanut oil and sesame oil over high heat. Add a dash of salt, the ginger, and scallion and stir-fry 30 seconds. Add the asparagus and bell pepper and stir-fry just until the asparagus begins to soften, about 2 minutes. Remove the vegetable mixture from the pan and arrange on top of the bean threads, placing them in a ring just inside the outer edge of the bean threads.

4 Heat the remaining 1 tablespoon peanut oil and 1 teaspoon sesame oil in the skillet. Add the turkey mixture and cook, stirring occasionally and breaking up any large lumps of meat, until the turkey is no longer pink, about 2 minutes. Spoon into the center of the bean threads and serve at once.

Known as **bean threads** or **cellophane noodles**, these gossamer, translucent filaments aren't noodles in the traditional sense because they're made from the starch of green mung beans. Sold in dried bundles, bean threads or cellophane noodles must be soaked briefly in hot water before use in most dishes, although presoaking isn't necessary when they're added to soups. You may also deep-fry them. Cellophane noodles are sold in many supermarkets and in Asian grocery stores. Other names for bean threads include vermicelli, Chinese vermicelli, harusame, and the poetic, glass noodles.

Prized by the ancient Greeks and Romans, **asparagus** continues to be thought of as the aristocrat of vegetables. Asparagus is one of the lily family's cultivated forms. The best time for fresh asparagus ranges from February through June, although it's available year-round. Select asparagus with crisp, straight stalks and tight buds, and consume it as soon as possible after purchase to enjoy optimum quality and flavor. To trim asparagus, snap off the tough ends and discard. If desired, peel the bottom third or half of each stalk with a vegetable peeler to get a more tender texture.

Asian-Style Shrimp, Cabbage & Noodle Sauté

Fast can mean many different things, but few can quibble with this definition: 15 minutes from start to finish. A number of convenience foods are called on as cohorts in this quick skillet dish that taps into several cuisines for its influences.

MAKES:
4 servings

PREP:
10 minutes

COOK:
5 minutes

2   **cups chicken stock or reduced-sodium canned broth**

2   **(3-ounce) packages ramen noodle soup mix, Oriental flavor**

2   **tablespoons vegetable oil**

1   **(16-ounce) package shredded cabbage or cole slaw mix**

6   **scallions, slivered**

8   **ounces small peeled shrimp, cooked and patted dry**

    Juice of 1 lime

1   **tablespoon peanut butter**

1   **tablespoon brown sugar**

¼   **teaspoon crushed hot red pepper, or more to taste**

½   **cup minced cilantro**

¼   **cup finely minced peanuts**

1 In a wok or large skillet, heat the stock to a simmer. Add the noodles (the seasoning packets will not be used in this recipe), breaking them up with a spoon. Cover and cook, stirring occasionally, until the noodles are softened and most of the liquid is absorbed, 3 to 4 minutes. Remove the noodles from the pan and set aside.

2 Add the oil to the wok and increase the heat to high. Add the cabbage and scallions and cook, stirring often, until the cabbage has wilted, 1 to 2 minutes.

3 Add the shrimp, lime juice, peanut butter, brown sugar, and hot pepper and cook just until heated through, 1 minute. Garnish with the cilantro and peanuts.

Turkey Posole

A big mound of leftover turkey served as the inspiration for this recipe, and it's one of the best ways ever to put a dent in the post-holiday supply. When there's no carcass to strip, leftover chicken or pork can be used, and other vegetables can be added, too. Corn, zucchini, and even bits of diced winter squash are all fine candidates.

MAKES:
3 to 4 servings

PREP:
10 minutes

STAND:
30 minutes

COOK:
20 minutes

1 Place the dried chili peppers in a small heatproof bowl and add enough boiling water just to cover. Let stand until the chili peppers are softened, at least 30 minutes. Remove and discard the stem and seeds, pat the chili peppers dry, and mince finely.

2 In a large saucepan, heat the oil over medium-high heat. Add the minced chili peppers and cumin and cook, stirring often, for 3 minutes. Add the onion and bell pepper and cook until the onion is softened, 8 to 10 minutes longer. Sprinkle the flour over the vegetable mixture. Cook, stirring, for 1 minute.

3 Stir in the remaining ingredients. Reduce the heat to low and simmer gently, uncovered, until slightly thickened, 8 to 10 minutes.

2	**dried guajillo or ancho chili peppers**
1½	**teaspoons olive or vegetable oil**
1	**teaspoon ground cumin**
1	**medium onion, chopped**
1	**red bell pepper, chopped**
1	**tablespoon flour**
3	**cups shredded cooked turkey**
1	**(15- to 16-ounce) can white hominy, drained**
1	**(10-ounce) can diced tomatoes with green chili peppers, juices reserved**
1	**cup chicken stock or reduced-sodium canned broth**
¼	**teaspoon salt**

Braises, simple casseroles, meltingly tender pot roasts, and the most succulent briskets are the defining essence of good, old-fashioned, home-style cooking. Sturdy and sustaining, these baked one-pot meals fill the house with their aromatic presence, tantalizing and tempting with the promise of a great meal in the making. For all of their simplicity, they are also filled with delicious contradictions. With an appealing roster of decidedly old-fashioned traits, they also come across as startlingly modern and up-to-date.

The best of the baked dishes harbor complex tastes and textures that rank them among some of the all-time greatest dishes. **Pot Roast with Caramelized Vegetables** takes a time-tested favorite and adds the new spin of separately cooked vegetables. **Beer & Chili Braised Beef Brisket** layers sweet, smoky, and hot tastes into a wonderful amalgamation of flavors. Characterized by their homespun charms, they also fit right into the relaxed rules of entertaining. For proof, turn to the **Rack of Lamb with Couscous, Roasted Fennel & Peppers** or the **Herbed Pork Roast with Balsamic-Glazed Potatoes & Red Onions**.

Dinner's in the Oven

Though many of these dishes ask for long, slow cooking to bring out their best attributes, most of the cooking time is unattended, leaving you free to indulge in other activities. And the adage about these dishes always tasting better the next day builds in the flexibility of cooking them ahead and reheating them briefly at serving time.

Oven-baked meals can be enjoyed all year. Cold, crisp salads filled with vibrantly fresh ingredients and a great loaf of bread make fine companions.

Greek Beef Stew with Macaroni

In many ways, this is similar to the classic beef stew recipes that fill recipe files and bring a homey touch to many a meal table. But only up to a point. The addition of warm sweet spices enhances the flavor of the stew and makes it distinctly and deliciously Greek in character.

MAKES:
4 to 6 servings

PREP:
15 minutes

COOK:
1 hour, 30 minutes

1 Preheat the oven to 350° F. In a large flameproof casserole, heat the olive oil over high heat. Add the meat in batches and cook, turning occasionally, until browned on all sides, 6 to 8 minutes per batch. Return all the beef to the pan.

2 Add the onions and garlic to the pan and cook, stirring often, until the onions begin to soften, about 5 minutes. Add the wine and stir up any browned bits from the bottom of the pan. Add all the remaining ingredients except the pasta.

3 Cover the casserole and transfer it to the oven. Bake until the beef is tender, 1 to 1¼ hours, stirring several times. Add the macaroni and mix lightly.

2	tablespoons olive oil
2	pounds beef chuck, cut into 1-inch cubes
3	small onions, peeled and quartered
1	garlic clove, minced
⅔	cup dry red wine
1	cup beef stock or reduced-sodium canned broth
3	tablespoons tomato paste
2	tablespoons red wine vinegar
1	tablespoon brown sugar
1	teaspoon dried oregano
1	teaspoon dried rosemary
1	teaspoon salt
¼	teaspoon cinnamon
¼	teaspoon ground cloves
¼	teaspoon freshly ground pepper
2	cups cooked elbow macaroni

Beer & Chili Braised Beef Brisket

Brisket can be a fatty cut of meat; refrigerating it overnight makes it easy to skim off the excess fat. The added bonus is that the meat, vegetables, and sauce all taste even better reheated.

MAKES:
8 to 10 servings

PREP:
15 minutes

COOK:
3 hours,
30 minutes

REFRIGERATE:
overnight

REHEAT:
1 hour to 1 hour,
30 minutes

2 garlic cloves, minced

¼ cup plus 1 tablespoon brown sugar

2 teaspoons ground cumin

1 teaspoon salt

½ teaspoon ground black pepper

¼ teaspoon cinnamon

5 pounds beef brisket

2 large onions, cut into wedges

1 cup dark beer or stout

3 tablespoons tomato paste

2 dried chipotle chili peppers

8 to 10 small red potatoes, cut in half

8 ounces baby carrots

1 Preheat the oven to 325° F. Line a 13 x 9-inch baking pan with heavy-duty aluminum foil, extending it about 3 inches beyond the sides.

2 In a small bowl, combine the garlic, 1 tablespoon of the brown sugar, the cumin, salt, pepper, and cinnamon. Stir to mix. Place the meat in the lined pan and rub the spice mixture all over the brisket. Scatter the onion wedges over the meat.

3 In a medium bowl, stir together the beer, tomato paste, and the remaining ¼ cup brown sugar. Pour over the meat and onions. Add the chili peppers. Cover with another piece of foil and crimp the edges so the meat is tightly wrapped.

4 Bake 2½ hours. Remove the top sheet of foil and spoon some of the pan juices over the meat. Bake 1 hour longer. Remove from the oven and cool slightly. Using a slotted spoon, remove the onions from the broth and place on top of the meat. Cover and refrigerate overnight.

5 To finish cooking, preheat the oven to 350° F. Scrape the fat off the juices in the baking pan. Add the potatoes and carrots to the pan. Bake, uncovered, until the meat and vegetables are tender, 1 to 1½ hours.

Herbed Pork Roast with Balsamic-Glazed Potatoes & Red Onions

Workdays usually dictate that slow-cooking roasts be dealt aside in favor of meats that cook more quickly. Pork loin is an especially succulent and flavorful choice, one that bakes to near perfection with minimal attention. The addition of vegetables makes it a meal.

MAKES:
6 to 8 servings
PREP:
15 minutes
COOK:
1 hour, 40 minutes
STAND:
10 minutes

1 In a small bowl, combine 1 tablespoon of the olive oil, the garlic, rosemary, tarragon, thyme, basil, and ¼ teaspoon of the salt. Use a small, pointed knife to make slits all over the roast. Fill each slit with some of the herb mixture. This can be done several hours in advance.

2 Preheat the oven to 375° F. In a shallow flameproof roasting pan, heat the remaining 2 tablespoons olive oil over medium-high heat. Add the pork roast and cook, turning, until browned all over, 7 to 10 minutes. Carefully pour in the wine, heat to a boil, and cook, stirring often, for 2 minutes. Add the potatoes and transfer to the oven.

3 Bake 1 hour. Add the onions, vinegar, and the remaining ¼ teaspoon salt, stirring well so the onions and potatoes are well coated with the pan juices. Season with pepper to taste. Bake until the internal temperature of the roast is 155° F, about 30 minutes longer. Let stand 10 minutes before slicing.

3	tablespoons olive oil
2	large garlic cloves, minced
2	teaspoons dried rosemary
2	teaspoons dried tarragon
2	teaspoons dried thyme
½	teaspoon dried basil
½	teaspoon salt
1	center-cut boneless pork loin roast (3 to 4 pounds), tied
¾	cup dry white wine
9	small red new potatoes, cut in half
3	medium red onions, cut into thin wedges
2½	tablespoons balsamic or red wine vinegar
	Freshly ground pepper

Pot Roast with Caramelized Vegetables

Two-step cooking turns an everyday pot roast into something special. A selection of seasonal vegetables is cooked over very high heat so their natural sugar begins to caramelize. Then the meat is baked until it's mouthwateringly tender and ready to be joined by the vegetables. The vegetables stay crisp, and each of the flavors remains distinct.

MAKES:
4 servings

PREP:
15 minutes

COOK:
1 hour,
50 minutes

2	tablespoons vegetable oil
½	teaspoon salt
½	of a medium rutabaga, peeled and cut into 1-inch cubes
1	large onion, halved crosswise and cut into ½-inch wedges
4	medium carrots, peeled and diagonally sliced 1 inch thick
1½	cups Brussels sprouts, cut in half

2	cups beef stock or reduced-sodium canned broth
½	teaspoon sugar

1	boneless beef chuck pot roast (about 1¾ pounds), patted dry

2	tablespoons tomato paste
2	bay leaves
2	whole allspice berries
1	teaspoon dried thyme leaves

Freshly ground pepper

1 In a large flameproof casserole, heat 1 tablespoon of the oil with ¼ teaspoon of the salt over high heat. Add the rutabaga, about ⅔ of the onion, three of the carrots, and the Brussels sprouts. Cook, stirring and shaking the pan almost constantly, until the vegetables begin to brown, 3 to 4 minutes. Cover, reduce the heat to medium, and cook, stirring frequently, 5 minutes longer.

2 Add ½ cup of the beef stock and the sugar. Cover and cook until the rutabaga begins to soften, 7 to 10 minutes. Remove the vegetables and any remaining stock to a bowl and set aside.

3 Preheat the oven to 325° F. Return the pan to high heat and add the remaining 1 tablespoon oil. Add the meat and cook, turning occasionally, until the meat is browned on both sides, 7 to 10 minutes, adding the remaining onion and carrot after 5 minutes.

4 Add the remaining beef stock and ¼ teaspoon salt, the tomato paste, bay leaves, allspice berries, and thyme. Bring to a boil.

5 Cover the pan and transfer to the oven. Bake until the meat is tender, about 1¼ hours. Skim the fat from the top of the pan juices. Add the reserved vegetables, stirring them so they are coated well with juices. Bake just until the vegetables are hot, 10 minutes longer. Season with pepper to taste.

Said to have been first cultivated in 16th-century Belgium, **Brussels sprouts** resemble tiny cabbage heads, and they are indeed members of the cabbage family. Many rows of sprouts grow on a single long stalk. Sold fresh or frozen, they range from 1 to 2 inches in diameter. Brussels sprouts are available year-round, but their peak season ranges from late August through March. If buying them fresh, choose small, bright green sprouts with compact heads. Right before cooking, trim brussels sprouts by removing any yellow or bruised leaves and slicing off the stem.

Available ground or dried whole, **allspice** is the dark brown, pea-size berry of the evergreen pimiento tree. Caribbean in origin with a flavor suggesting a blend of cinnamon, cloves, and nutmeg, allspice is used in both savory and sweet cooking. The liqueurs Benedictine and Chartreuse include allspice as an ingredient, as do many holiday sweets, and Scandinavian herring dishes. Jamaica provides most of the world's supply, and accordingly allspice is also called Jamaican pepper, Jamaican spice, or English spice.

Cornbread-Stuffed Pork Chops with Vidalia Onion Sauce

The old-fashioned hominess of stuffed pork chops gets glorious treatment here with a sweet onion sauce and a generous dose of bourbon.

MAKES:
4 servings

PREP:
10 minutes

COOK:
1 hour, 35 minutes

2	large Vidalia onions
4	bacon slices, chopped
1	small tart apple, unpeeled, cored and diced
½	teaspoon dried thyme
½	teaspoon dried sage
½	teaspoon salt
¼	teaspoon freshly ground pepper
¼	cup plus 3 tablespoons bourbon
1	cup packaged cornbread stuffing mix
1	egg, lightly beaten
2 to 3	tablespoons milk
4	pork loin chops on the bone, cut 1¼ inches thick
2	tablespoons unsalted butter
½	cup chicken stock or reduced-sodium canned broth
⅓	cup heavy cream
2	tablespoons minced fresh chives

1 Preheat the oven to 350° F. Finely chop about one-quarter of one of the onions. Slice the rest.

2 In a large ovenproof skillet, cook the bacon over medium heat until it is browned, about 5 minutes. Add the chopped onion and cook over high heat, stirring often, until the onion is softened, 4 to 5 minutes.

3 Add the apple, thyme, sage, ¼ teaspoon of the salt, and ⅛ teaspoon pepper. Cook, stirring occasionally, 2 minutes. Add 3 tablespoons of the bourbon and cook, stirring, until it has evaporated, 2 to 3 minutes.

4 Stir in the cornbread stuffing mix, and cook 1 minute. Transfer to a medium bowl and let cool slightly. Stir in the egg and enough milk to make a moist but not wet mixture.

5 Carefully cut a pocket in each pork chop, going all the way to the bone. Fill each pocket with stuffing, dividing it evenly among the four chops.

6 Wipe out the skillet. Add the butter and melt it over high heat. Add the sliced onions; cook, stirring often, until they are golden, 5 to 6 minutes. Carefully add the remaining ¼ cup bourbon and cook until it has evaporated, 2 to 3 minutes. Add the chicken stock and remove the pan from the heat.

7 Arrange the pork chops in the skillet and cover loosely with foil. Bake 40 minutes. Turn the chops over and continue to bake, uncovered, until they are tender, 20 to 30 minutes longer.

8 Transfer the pork chops to a platter and tent with foil to keep warm. Bring the contents of the skillet to a boil on top of the stove and cook until slightly thickened, 3 minutes. Add the cream and the remaining ¼ teaspoon salt and ⅛ teaspoon pepper. Bring to a boil and cook 2 minutes. Pour over the chops and sprinkle with the chives.

Vidalia onions have brown skins, a crisp texture, and sweet, juicy white flesh that tastes great raw. The onions also can be cooked, and their delicate flavor doesn't overpower other foods. More than 60 years ago, farmers near Vidalia, Georgia, noticed that the soil and climate of this particular region matures these onions into a gourmet delight. In 1990, the Georgia State Legislature named the Vidalia its Official State Vegetable. Requiring an eight-month growing period, the onions are usually harvested just once a year, from May through June.

Bourbon is a respected American whiskey distilled from fermented grain. To be called bourbon, the whiskey must be made primarily from corn and produced in Kentucky. Aged in oak barrels for at least two years, bourbon has a deep caramel color and a somewhat sweet, smoky taste.

Stuffed Cabbage Rolls

These leafy little bundles are packed with the perfect blend of savory ingredients, including rice, pork, ham, and cabbage. Prunes add a sweet note that is balanced by mustard and spices. Select a large head of cabbage with big, loose leaves still attached—the best ones for filling.

MAKES:
4 to 6 servings

PREP:
30 minutes

COOK:
45 minutes

1	large head of green or Savoy cabbage, large outer leaves intact

2	tablespoons vegetable oil
2	medium onions, chopped
2	garlic cloves, minced

1	pound ground pork
1/2	cup finely chopped smoked ham
1	cup cooked converted long-grain white rice
1/3	cup finely chopped pitted prunes
2	teaspoons Dijon mustard
2	teaspoons Hungarian sweet paprika
3/4	teaspoon dried thyme leaves
1/4	teaspoon dried tarragon
1/4	teaspoon ground allspice
1/4	teaspoon salt
1/2	teaspoon freshly ground pepper

1	(14 1/2-ounce) can stewed tomatoes
1	tablespoon brown sugar

1 Remove 8 to 10 large outer leaves from the cabbage. Arrange the leaves on a baking sheet and freeze until solid. Remove the leaves from the freezer and let stand at room temperature to soften so they can be rolled. Preheat the oven to 325° F. Have a large, shallow baking dish ready.

2 Finely chop 2 cups of cabbage from the remaining head of cabbage and place in a large bowl.

3 In a large skillet, heat the oil over medium heat. Add the onions and garlic. Cook over medium heat, stirring often, until the onions begin to soften, about 5 minutes. Add the onions to the chopped cabbage along with the ground pork, ham, rice, prunes, mustard, paprika, thyme, tarragon, allspice, salt, and 1/4 teaspoon of the pepper. Mix thoroughly.

4 Divide the filling among eight of the best-looking cabbage leaves, spooning it into a mound in the center. Roll up each cabbage leaf to form a neat, fully encased bundle and place in the baking dish, seam-side down.

5 Place the tomatoes, brown sugar, and remaining 1/4 teaspoon pepper in a blender or food processor. Puree until smooth. Pour the sauce over the cabbage rolls, cover with aluminum foil, and bake 45 minutes, or until they are heated through.

Roasted Vegetable Stew

A bountiful collection of vegetables is roasted first with herbs, garlic, and oil, then with a final addition of marinara sauce. Even though it may appear to have a wintry demeanor, this stew is a fine summer dish, served at room temperature.

MAKES:
4 to 6 servings

PREP:
25 minutes

DRAIN:
30 minutes

COOK:
50 minutes

1 Place the eggplant in a colander, sprinkle with ½ teaspoon salt, and toss lightly to coat. Let drain for 30 minutes, then wrap in several thicknesses of paper towels. Squeeze gently to remove as much moisture as possible.

2 Combine the eggplant, celery, bell pepper, potatoes, zucchini, fennel, and onion in a 13 x 9-inch roasting pan. In a small bowl, mix the olive oil, garlic, basil, hot red pepper, and remaining ¼ teaspoon salt. Pour over the vegetables and toss to coat. Bake at 350° F for 30 minutes.

3 Pour the wine over the vegetable mixture, and stir. Add the marinara sauce and stir again. Return to the oven and bake 20 minutes longer. Remove from the oven, stir in the vinegar, and sprinkle the Parmesan cheese on top.

1	large eggplant, peeled and cut into 1-inch cubes
¾	teaspoon salt
2	celery ribs, diagonally sliced 1 inch thick
1	red or green bell pepper, cut into 1-inch squares
2	medium yellow or red potatoes, scrubbed and cut into ½-inch dice
1	medium zucchini, quartered lengthwise and cut crosswise into ¾-inch-thick slices
1	small fennel bulb, cut into ¾-inch dice, or 1¼ cups sliced celery
1	medium onion, cut into ¾-inch dice
2	tablespoons olive oil
1	large garlic clove, minced
1	teaspoon dried basil
¼	teaspoon crushed hot red pepper
¼	cup dry white wine
1¼	cups marinara or spaghetti sauce
1¼	teaspoons balsamic or red wine vinegar
¼	cup grated Parmesan cheese

Gypsy Goulash

This is a combination of two classic styles of goulash, borrowing the best from both. The finished dish is a stew-like casserole. The sauerkraut adds a bit of texture as well as an unexpected taste, a subtle tang that plays off the richness of the broth.

MAKES:
6 servings

PREP:
25 minutes

COOK:
1 hour, 50 minutes

2	bacon slices, diced
1	large onion, chopped

1¼	pounds pork shoulder, cut into 1-inch cubes
½	pound veal or beef stew meat, cut into 1-inch cubes

2	tablespoons Hungarian sweet paprika
½	teaspoon caraway seeds
½	cup dry white wine

3	medium yellow or red potatoes, cut into 1-inch chunks
2	small green bell peppers, cut into 1-inch squares
1⅓	cups chicken stock or reduced-sodium canned broth
1¼	cups cold-pack sauerkraut, rinsed and squeezed dry

1	large tomato, diced
½	cup sour cream
	Salt and freshly ground pepper

1 Preheat the oven to 350° F. In a large flameproof casserole, cook the bacon with the onions over medium heat, stirring occasionally, until the bacon is crisp, 5 to 7 minutes. Add the pork and veal in two batches and cook, stirring occasionally, until the meats are no longer pink, 6 to 8 minutes per batch. Return all the meat to the pan.

2 Sprinkle with the paprika and caraway seeds. Add the wine and cook 1 minute. Add the potatoes, bell peppers, chicken stock, and sauerkraut.

3 Cover tightly and transfer the casserole to the oven. Bake until the meat and potatoes are tender, about 1½ hours. Stir in the tomato and sour cream and season with salt and pepper to taste just before serving.

Tandoori-Style Game Hens

Tandoors *are clay ovens used in Indian cooking, while* tandoori *describes the mix of yogurt and spices that is often used on foods cooked in these ovens. It lends an aromatic taste to hens and sweet potatoes alike. Depending on appetites and the rest of the meal, some people may be satisfied with half a hen for a serving. In this case, cut them in half with kitchen shears before adding them to the marinade. The cooking time will be slightly less for the halves, about 40 minutes.*

MAKES:
2 to 4 servings
PREP:
15 minutes
MARINADE:
12 to 24 hours
COOK:
45 minutes

1 | Place the onion, garlic, and ginger in a food processor. Puree until smooth. Add the yogurt, lemon juice, coriander, paprika, cayenne, turmeric, salt, cardamom, and allspice. Blend well. Transfer to a large plastic food storage bag, and add the hens. Seal the bag tightly and refrigerate 12 to 24 hours.

2 | Preheat the oven to 450° F. Remove the hens from the marinade, letting any excess drip off. Arrange the hens, breast-side up, in a shallow roasting pan. Scatter the sweet potatoes around the hens and brush with some of the remaining marinade. Bake 45 to 50 minutes, or until the juices from the thighs run clear, brushing the hens with the marinade several times during the first 35 minutes. Sprinkle the scallions over the hens and sweet potatoes, and serve.

1 **small onion, quartered**
1 **large garlic clove**
1 **(1-inch) piece of fresh ginger**

1 **cup plain yogurt**
¼ **cup fresh lemon juice**
1 **teaspoon ground coriander**
1 **teaspoon Hungarian sweet paprika**
¼ **teaspoon cayenne**
¼ **teaspoon ground turmeric**
¼ **teaspoon salt**
⅛ **teaspoon ground cardamom**
⅛ **teaspoon ground allspice**

2 **Cornish game hens, rinsed and patted dry**

2 **small sweet potatoes, cut into 1½-inch chunks**

2 **scallions, sliced**

Rack of Lamb with Couscous, Roasted Fennel & Peppers

Rack of lamb is a costly and dear cut of meat, best reserved for special occasions, perhaps when there's romance on the menu.

MAKES:
2 servings

PREP:
10 minutes

COOK:
1 hour

1 **medium fennel bulb, trimmed and cut into ¾-inch dice**

1 **medium red bell pepper, cut into ¾-inch dice**

2 **tablespoons dry white wine or vermouth**

1 **tablespoon olive oil**

½ **teaspoon salt**

¼ **teaspoon freshly ground pepper**

2 **teaspoons Dijon mustard**

1 **rack of lamb with 4 ribs (about 1½ to 1¾ pounds)**

½ **cup couscous**

Pinch of cayenne

2 **scallions, sliced**

1 Preheat the oven to 425° F. In a 9-inch gratin pan or other small, shallow roasting pan, combine the fennel, bell pepper, wine, olive oil, ¼ teaspoon of the salt, and the pepper. Toss so the vegetables are well coated. Cover and bake 30 minutes.

2 Spread the mustard over the rounded, meaty side of the lamb. Place the lamb atop the vegetables in the pan. Bake, uncovered, 25 minutes, or until the internal temperature of the lamb is 125° to 130° F for rare. Transfer the lamb to a platter and tent with foil.

3 Add the couscous, ½ cup boiling water, and the remaining ¼ teaspoon salt to the vegetables in the pan. Mix lightly. Cover the pan and bake 5 minutes longer. Add the cayenne and scallions and fluff with a fork. Cut the lamb into ribs and serve with the couscous.

Rosemary Roast Chicken with Fennel & Peppers

Adapted from a regional Italian recipe originally made with rabbit, this rousing version proves that chicken is just as successful.

MAKES:
3 to 4 servings

PREP:
20 minutes

MARINADE:
4 to 12 hours

COOK:
1 hour

1 Preheat the oven to 400° F. In a small bowl, combine the garlic, 2 tablespoons of the rosemary, the sage, ¼ teaspoon of the salt, and ¼ teaspoon of the pepper to make a paste. Rub the paste over the chicken pieces, cover, and refrigerate 4 to 12 hours.

2 In a large, shallow flameproof roasting pan, arrange the chicken, skin-side up, the fennel, and the bell pepper. Scatter the pancetta over the ingredients in the pan. Sprinkle with the olive oil, lemon juice, and remaining ¼ teaspoon salt and ¼ teaspoon pepper. Bake 30 minutes. Pour the chicken stock into the bottom of the pan and bake until the juices from the chicken thighs run clear, 25 to 30 minutes longer.

3 Transfer the chicken and vegetables to a large platter and cover to keep warm. Place the pan over high heat and add the wine. Stir up the browned bits from the bottom of the pan and boil until the juices are slightly reduced, 2 to 3 minutes. Add the remaining 1 tablespoon rosemary, and adjust the seasoning. Pour over the chicken and vegetables and serve.

1 **large garlic clove, forced through a press or minced very finely**

3 **tablespoons minced fresh rosemary**

2 **teaspoons minced fresh sage**

½ **teaspoon salt**

½ **teaspoon freshly ground pepper**

1 **large frying chicken (about 3½ pounds), cut into serving pieces**

1 **large fennel bulb, trimmed and cut into 1-inch wedges**

1 **large red or yellow bell pepper, diced**

2 **ounces pancetta, finely diced, or ½ cup diced bacon**

2 **tablespoons olive oil**
  Juice of ½ of a medium lemon

⅔ **cup chicken stock or reduced-sodium canned broth**

¼ **cup dry white wine**

King Ranch Casserole

This wickedly rich casserole is a Texas tradition, showing up at buffet dinners of practically every type. Canned soups have always been a traditional part of the formula; here, they have been replaced by prepared Alfredo sauce. For even more ease, this is a great opportunity to rely on the convenience of a rotisserie chicken from the market.

MAKES:
6 servings

PREP:
20 minutes

COOK:
30 minutes

STAND:
5 minutes

Meat from 1 cooked frying chicken, pulled into large shreds

1   small onion, diced

1   small red bell pepper, roasted (see page 33) and finely diced

1   small poblano or green bell pepper, roasted and finely diced

1   (10-ounce) can diced tomatoes with chili peppers, juices reserved

1   (10-ounce) container prepared Alfredo sauce

1   cup chicken stock or reduced-sodium canned broth

½   cup milk

⅛ to ¼   teaspoon cayenne, or more to taste

10   corn tortillas

2   cups shredded cheese, such as Chihuahua, Monterey Jack, or a dry goat cheese

Optional garnishes: diced avocado, diced tomato, sliced scallions

1 Preheat the oven to 350° F. In a medium bowl, combine the chicken, onion, and roasted peppers. In a separate medium bowl, combine the tomatoes with their juices, the Alfredo sauce, chicken stock, milk, and cayenne. Mix well.

2 Place a layer of tortillas in a 3- to 4-quart casserole. Layer evenly with some of the chicken mixture, sauce mixture, and cheese. Continue layering, ending up with a layer of cheese on top.

3 Bake 30 to 35 minutes, or until heated through. Let stand 5 minutes before serving. Top with garnishes as desired.

Tuna, Broccoli & Brie Casserole

Culinary prominence may not be in the stars for tuna casseroles, but they are an integral part of American cookery. With absolutely no pretensions or aspirations for anything more than satisfying a hungry soul, they've carved out and maintained a steady hold within their niche. This one dispenses with the whole ritual of canned soups, instead looking to fresh vegetables and ultra-creamy Brie cheese for a surprising new twist.

MAKES:
3 to 4 servings
PREP:
10 minutes
COOK:
40 minutes

1 Preheat the oven to 350° F. In a medium flameproof casserole, cook the pasta according to the package directions, adding the broccoli to the water about 5 minutes before the pasta is fully cooked.

2 Drain well and return the pasta mixture to the casserole. While the mixture is hot, add the onion and cheese, stirring lightly to melt the cheese. Add the milk and mustard; stir to blend. Mix in the scallions, roasted pepper, tuna, salt, and pepper.

3 Transfer to the oven and bake about 30 minutes, or until the mixture is bubbly, stirring once halfway through. Stir in the tomato just before serving.

8	ounces penne or fusilli
1	large broccoli stalk, coarsely chopped
1	small onion, minced
6	ounces Brie cheese, with the rind removed
1½	cups milk
½	teaspoon Dijon mustard
4	scallions, sliced
½	cup diced roasted red pepper
1	(6½-ounce) can solid white tuna packed in water, drained and flaked
½	teaspoon salt
¼	teaspoon freshly ground pepper
1	plum tomato, finely diced

Peruvian-Spiced Baked Fish with Quinoa

Quinoa, an ancient grain that grows high on the peaks of the Andes mountains, forms a substantive base for a colorful medley of tomato and pepper-topped fish fillets. High in protein and possessing a delicate, nutty taste, quinoa can be found in health food stores and well-stocked supermarkets.

MAKES:
4 servings

PREP:
15 minutes

COOK:
40 minutes

1   tablespoon annatto seeds

¼   cup olive oil

1   shallot, minced

1   cup quinoa, rinsed well under cold water

1   teaspoon grated orange zest
½   teaspoon ground cumin

¾   teaspoon salt
     Freshly ground pepper

4   firm, white-fleshed fish fillets, such as scrod, Chilean bass, or snapper (about 6 ounces each)

1   small red onion, halved and thinly sliced

1   garlic clove, minced

4   large ripe tomatoes (about 2 pounds), seeded and chopped, or 1 (28-ounce) can peeled plum tomatoes, well drained and coarsely chopped

1   cup minced cilantro

1 In a large, deep-sided, ovenproof sauté pan or flameproof casserole, place the annatto seeds and cook over high heat, stirring frequently, until the seeds are fragrant, 45 to 60 seconds. Reduce the heat to low, add the olive oil, and cook until the oil is golden-colored, 4 to 5 minutes, making sure the oil doesn't begin to smoke. Strain the oil and discard the seeds.

2 Preheat the oven to 375° F. Return 2 tablespoons of the strained oil to the pan, and heat over low heat. Add the shallot and cook, stirring often, until it begins to soften, 2 to 3 minutes. Add the quinoa and cook, stirring often, until it begins to smell toasted, 1 to 2 minutes.

3 Add 1¾ cups water, the orange zest, and cumin, and bring to a boil over high heat. Reduce the heat to low and simmer until the liquid is absorbed, 12 to 15 minutes. Season with half of the salt and pepper to taste.

4 Arrange the fish on top of the quinoa. In a medium bowl, combine the onion, garlic, tomatoes, and cilantro, and stir lightly. Spoon atop the fish and drizzle with the remaining strained olive oil. Season with the remaining salt and pepper to taste.

5 Cover the pan, transfer to the oven, and bake 15 minutes. Uncover and continue to bake until the fish is no longer opaque in the center, 5 to 10 minutes longer.

Annatto seeds, also called *achiote*, are available in Latin American groceries and some large supermarkets. If they aren't available, omit them, adding a pinch of ground turmeric, if desired, for color.

White-fleshed fish denotes those that have their fat concentrated in the liver, not the flesh. These lean fish, with less than 2 percent fat in the flesh, include sole, flounder, halibut, and cod. Don't confuse this term with whitefish, the common name of members of the *Salmonidae* species.

There may never be enough ways to prepare chicken and turkey to satisfy the ever-increasing appetite for these lean birds. Favored for lots of good reasons, including ease, economy, health, and versatility, both chicken and turkey continue to carve out prominent places at the meal table. Now, they often form the basis of the most preferred meals, both plain and fancy. Recipes such as **Braised Chicken & Vegetables with Ginger-Lime Broth & Couscous** and **Chicken Pot au Feu** show the dressed-up side, while **Fricasseed Chicken with Garden Herbs & Vegetables**, **Turkey Breast with Stewed Barley & Leek Pilaf**, and **Chicken Stew with Rice & Spring Vegetables** play up tastes that are familiar and comforting.

Both chicken and turkey are relatively mild in flavor. This subtlety can be deliciously exploited by cooking them with a collection of bold and sassy spices. Almost all of the world's cuisines use chicken in one way or another, so many cultural influences show up in this chapter, taking chicken well beyond the realm of humdrum dining. **Basque-Style Chicken**; **Down Island Chicken & Turnip Stew**; and **Colombian Chicken, Potato & Avocado Stew** are just a few of the foreign accents that are served up so well with chicken.

Chicken & Turkey for Dinner

Almost all of the recipes offer the option of cooking poultry without the skin. This cuts down on fat, making lean fowl even leaner and more appealing. All the recipes can be made ahead of time and reheated, but be sure not to overcook them so they remain vibrant and appealing.

Several of the recipes in this chapter take advantage of the rotisserie chickens that are now sold in almost all supermarkets. Fully cooked and ready to go, they're timewise alternatives to buying and roasting a chicken. But if the grill is fired up, add an extra chicken or two to have on hand for recipes that call for cooked chicken.

Chicken Stew with Rice & Spring Vegetables

There's a strong resemblance to arroz con pollo *in this low-fat offering. Boneless chicken thighs are increasingly available at supermarkets, priced considerably lower than chicken breasts. If you can't find them, use the same part with the bone in, although be sure to remove the skin and trim away the excess fat.*

MAKES:
4 to 5 servings

PREP:
15 minutes

COOK:
30 minutes

STAND:
5 minutes

1 In a large, deep nonstick sauté pan or flameproof casserole, heat the olive oil over medium-high heat. Add the chicken and cook, turning, until browned on both sides, 6 to 8 minutes. Remove the chicken and set aside. Add the onion, garlic, thyme, coriander, and turmeric to the pan, reduce the heat to medium, and cook, stirring often, until the onion softens, about 5 minutes.

2 Add the rice and stir well. Pour in the chicken stock, salt, and pepper. Return the chicken to the pan, cover, and bring to a boil. Reduce the heat to medium-low and simmer gently 15 minutes.

3 Add the bell pepper, tomatoes, peas, and asparagus. Cover and continue to cook until the vegetables are crisp-tender, 5 to 8 minutes. Remove the pan from the heat and let stand, covered, 5 minutes. Serve, garnished with the parsley.

1	tablespoon olive oil
8	skinless, boneless chicken thighs (about 1¼ pounds)
1	medium onion, chopped
1	large garlic clove, minced
¾	teaspoon dried thyme leaves
¾	teaspoon ground coriander
¼	teaspoon ground turmeric
1	cup converted long-grain white rice
2½	cups chicken stock or reduced-sodium canned broth
1	teaspoon salt
¼	teaspoon freshly ground pepper
1	small red bell pepper, diced
2	large plum tomatoes, diced
½	cup tiny frozen peas
¼	pound slender asparagus, cut into 1-inch pieces

Minced parsley or fresh chervil

Basque-Style Chicken

There's a delightful peasant quality to this Spanish recipe, with smoky ham,
briny olives, and sweet peppers all adding rustic nuances to the chicken.
The dish reheats nicely, so it can be made ahead.

MAKES:
3 to 4 servings
PREP:
20 minutes
COOK:
45 minutes

1½   tablespoons olive oil

1   large frying chicken (3¼ pounds),
cut into serving pieces

1   large red bell pepper, cut into
1-inch squares

1   large green bell pepper, cut into
1-inch squares

2   medium onions, cut into thin wedges

¼   pound small mushrooms
(halved or quartered)

¼   pound smoked ham, diced (about 1 cup)

2   tablespoons sherry vinegar
or white wine vinegar

2   large tomatoes, diced

⅓   cup chicken broth

2   teaspoons minced fresh marjoram
or 1 teaspoon dried

½   teaspoon salt

⅛   teaspoon cayenne

⅓   cup ripe olives

3   tablespoons tomato paste

1 In a nonreactive Dutch oven, heat the oil over medium-high heat. Add the chicken and cook, turning, until browned on both sides, 8 to 10 minutes. Remove the chicken from the pan, and set aside.

2 Add the bell peppers, onions, mushrooms, and ham to the pan and cook over medium-high heat, stirring often, until the peppers begin to soften, 4 to 5 minutes. Pour in the vinegar and stir up any browned bits from the bottom of the pan. Add the tomatoes, chicken broth, marjoram, salt, and cayenne.

3 Reduce the heat to medium-low, cover, and cook gently until the chicken is tender and no longer pink in the center, 30 to 35 minutes. Transfer the chicken and vegetables to a platter and keep warm.

4 Add the olives and tomato paste to the pan juices. Boil, uncovered, until slightly thickened, 2 to 3 minutes. Pour the sauce over the chicken.

Don't mistake **marjoram** for its close relative oregano, which is sometimes called wild marjoram. Marjoram is sweeter and milder than oregano. A member of the mint family, this herb was often placed on the graves of the ancient Greeks to symbolize happiness in this existence and in the afterlife. It's used to season meats (particularly lamb), poultry, seafood, vegetables, and eggs, and works best when added near the end of the cooking period (otherwise, its flavor dissipates).

Raw **olives** must be cured before they can be eaten, and the curing medium—usually brine, lye, or salt—affects both flavor and texture, as does the degree of ripeness when the olive was picked. Green olives are picked while unripe. This makes them denser and more bitter than brown or black olives, which stay on the tree until fully ripe. You may purchase large, pitted mild black olives in cans. Stronger flavored cured black olives are sold by the pound, and in bottles or cans. Olives become bitter if they're cooked too long, so always add them to hot dishes at the last minute.

To pit olives easily, press them with the flat side of a chef's knife, roll them a bit with the blade, and then remove the pits.

Braised Chicken & Vegetables with Ginger-Lime Broth & Couscous

Sprightly tastes abound, from zesty lime to the quiet warmth that comes from the slightest hint of cinnamon. Vegetables added toward the end of cooking keep their color and crisp textures.

MAKES:
3 to 4 servings

PREP:
20 minutes

COOK:
55 minutes

3 tablespoons olive oil

1 medium onion, chopped

1 large garlic clove, minced

1 large piece of fresh ginger (about a 1½-inch cube), minced

1 small dried hot red pepper

1 medium bunch of cilantro, stems and leaves separated

1 cinnamon stick

1 (3-inch) piece of lime zest, removed with a vegetable peeler

3 cups chicken stock or reduced-sodium canned broth

1 large frying chicken (about 3½ pounds), quartered

½ teaspoon salt

¼ teaspoon freshly ground black pepper

1 cup couscous

¼ pound sugar snap peas, trimmed

1 plum tomato, diced

2 scallions, sliced

1 In a large heavy skillet, heat 1 tablespoon of the olive oil over medium heat. Add the onion, garlic, and ginger. Cook, stirring occasionally, until the onion is softened, about 5 minutes. Stir in the hot pepper, cilantro stems, cinnamon stick, and lime zest. Add the chicken stock, increase the heat to high, and bring to a boil. Boil, uncovered, until the liquid is reduced by about half, approximately 15 minutes. Strain and set aside.

2 Heat the remaining 2 tablespoons olive oil in the same skillet over medium-high heat. Season the chicken with the salt and black pepper and add to the pan. Cover tightly, reduce the heat to low, and cook gently, turning once or twice, until the chicken is tender and no longer pink in the center, 30 to 35 minutes. Transfer the chicken to a platter and cover to keep warm.

3 Heat the reserved broth. Place the couscous in a medium bowl and pour 1 cup of the hot broth over it. Cover and let stand 5 minutes. Meanwhile, add the sugar snap peas to the skillet and cook over high heat, stirring often, until the peas are just tender, 3 to 4 minutes. Using a slotted spoon, transfer the peas to the platter with the chicken. Sprinkle the tomatoes, scallions, and cilantro leaves over the chicken. Moisten the chicken with the remaining broth and serve with the couscous.

Cinnamon is widely used in sweet dishes, but also adds an intriguing element to savory stews and curries. It is the inner bark of a tropical evergreen tree, harvested during the rainy season when it's more pliable. As it dries, it curls into long quills, which are either ground into powder or cut into lengths and sold as cinnamon sticks. Once used in love potions and to perfume wealthy Romans, this age-old spice comes in two varieties, Ceylon cinnamon and cassia cinnamon. The first type is buff colored and mildly sweet in flavor while the second is dark, reddish brown with a more pungent, slightly bittersweet taste.

Fricasseed Chicken with Garden Herbs & Vegetables

A fricassee is catchall French term meaning stew. It implies a meat dish, most often chicken but also veal, rabbit, or Cornish game hens, simmered in gravy.

MAKES:
3 to 4 servings

PREP:
15 minutes

COOK:
50 minutes

2 tablespoons unsalted butter

1 large frying chicken (about 3½ pounds), cut into serving pieces

½ teaspoon salt

¼ teaspoon freshly ground pepper

2 tablespoons flour

2 cups chicken stock or reduced-sodium canned broth

2 teaspoons minced fresh tarragon or 1 teaspoon dried

2 teaspoons minced fresh rosemary or 1 teaspoon dried

2 small leeks, trimmed and cut into 1-inch lengths

2 large carrots, peeled and cut into 1-inch lengths

2 large celery ribs, cut into 1-inch lengths

1½ cups Brussels sprouts, cut in half if large

2 tablespoons minced parsley

2 tablespoons heavy cream

1 In a large skillet, melt the butter over medium-high heat. Add the chicken and season with some of the salt and pepper. Cook, turning occasionally, until browned on both sides, 8 to 10 minutes. Pour off all but about 2 tablespoons of fat from the pan. Sprinkle the flour into the skillet, then add the chicken stock, tarragon, rosemary, leeks, carrots, celery, and Brussels sprouts.

2 Cover the skillet and reduce the heat to medium-low. Simmer gently until the chicken is no longer pink in the center and the vegetables are tender, 35 to 40 minutes.

3 Transfer the chicken and vegetables to a serving platter and sprinkle with parsley. Skim the fat from the pan juices and boil, uncovered, until slightly thickened, 4 to 5 minutes. Stir in the cream and the remaining salt and pepper. Moisten the chicken and vegetables with a small amount of the sauce, and pass the rest at table.

Down Island Chicken & Turnip Stew

Caribbean influences infuse this simple, golden-yellow stew. Turnips add an earthy flavor that harmonizes nicely with the heat and spices. Boniato, a tuberous tropical vegetable, or sweet potatoes can be used in place of the turnips.

MAKES:
3 to 4 servings

PREP:
15 minutes

COOK:
45 minutes

1 In a large soup pot, melt 1½ tablespoons of the butter over medium-high heat. Add the chicken and cook, turning, until browned on both sides, 8 to 10 minutes.

2 Sprinkle the ginger and habañero pepper over the chicken. Stir in the curry powder, turmeric, allspice, cardamom, and salt. Mix well. Add the turnips, onions, and ½ cup chicken stock.

3 Cover and simmer gently until the chicken is tender and no longer pink in the center, 35 to 40 minutes. Add the remaining ¼ cup stock if the dish becomes too dry. Swirl in the remaining 1 tablespoon butter and serve over rice.

2½   **tablespoons unsalted butter**

1   **large frying chicken (about 3½ pounds), cut into serving pieces**

1   **piece of fresh ginger (about a 1-inch cube), minced**

1   **fresh habañero, jalapeño, or serrano pepper, seeded and minced**

1   **tablespoon curry powder**

1   **teaspoon ground turmeric**

¼   **teaspoon ground allspice**

¼   **teaspoon ground cardamom**

¼   **teaspoon salt**

3   **small turnips, peeled and cut into ½-inch cubes**

2   **medium onions, cut into ½-inch wedges**

¾   **cup chicken stock or reduced-sodium canned broth**

2   **cups cooked rice**

Chicken Paprikash

Hungarian cuisine allows for many variants on paprikash, some made with pork, others with beef or veal. Made with chicken, it is lighter and leaner, especially if the skin is removed from the chicken before it is cooked. The sour cream can be omitted, too, although it adds a sumptuously rich finish.

MAKES:
4 servings

PREP:
15 minutes

COOK:
55 minutes

1½ tablespoons vegetable oil, chicken fat, or rendered lard

½ pound smoked sausage, sliced 1 inch thick

1 large frying chicken (3½ pounds), cut into serving pieces and skin removed, if desired

1 teaspoon salt

¼ teaspoon freshly ground pepper

2 medium onions, halved crosswise and cut into ½-inch wedges

1 large green bell pepper, cut into 1-inch squares

6 small red potatoes, cut in half

2 tablespoons Hungarian sweet paprika

¼ teaspoon caraway seeds

½ cup dry white wine

1 cup chicken stock or reduced-sodium canned broth

1 large tomato, diced

¾ cup sour cream

2 tablespoons flour

1 In a large skillet, heat the oil over medium-high heat. Add the sausage and cook, turning occasionally, until well browned, 5 to 6 minutes. Remove the sausage from the pan and set aside.

2 Add the chicken pieces to the pan and season with ½ teaspoon of the salt and the pepper. Cook, turning, until browned on both sides, 8 to 10 minutes. Remove the chicken from the pan and set aside with the sausage.

3 Add the onions, bell pepper, and potatoes to the skillet. Cook, stirring often, until the onions begin to brown, 4 to 5 minutes. Add the paprika, caraway, and the remaining ½ teaspoon salt. Stir well and cook 1 minute.

4 Add the wine and stir up the browned bits from the bottom of the pan. Boil until almost all the wine has cooked away, 2 to 3 minutes. Add the chicken stock, tomato, chicken, and sausage. Reduce the heat to medium-low, cover, and simmer gently until the chicken is tender and no longer pink in the center, 30 to 35 minutes.

5 In a small bowl, combine the sour cream and the flour, mixing until smooth. Add to the pan, stirring well to combine. Heat to just below a boil and cook 1 minute, stirring constantly.

Paprika is used both as a spice and a garnish in a variety of dishes. Ground from the dried flesh of the paprika chili pepper, its color ranges from burnt orange to deep red. Paprika's taste can vary widely from sweet to pungent and mild to hot, with the standard grocery store variety generally mild. If you wish for a more powerful taste, specialty and gourmet shops have a greater selection. There will usually be a taste guide printed on the label of any prepackaged paprika.

Although Hungary is the country most often associated with this spice—it is, in fact, their national spice and a staple in Hungarian cuisine—Spain, Portugal, and California produce much commercial paprika. Sweet or hot Hungarian paprika is more pungent than the mild Spanish type, and recipes that call for paprika usually mean the Hungarian variety.

Italian Chicken & Sausage with Rice & Seared Peppers

*A salad of fennel and Parmesan cheese and lots of rustic
Italian bread are good partners to this hearty dish.*

MAKES:
3 to 4 servings
PREP:
10 minutes
COOK:
55 minutes

2 teaspoons olive oil

½ pound Italian sausage, cut into 4 pieces

1 large frying chicken (about 3½ pounds),
cut up and skinned

2 tablespoons red wine vinegar

1 large onion, diced

4 Italian frying peppers or 2 small green
bell peppers, cut into ¾-inch-wide strips

¾ cup converted long-grain white rice

1 (14½-ounce) can diced tomatoes,
juices reserved

1 cup chicken stock or reduced-sodium
canned broth

1 teaspoon dried basil

½ teaspoon dried oregano
Crushed hot red pepper

Salt

1 In a large, heavy soup pot, heat the oil over medium-high heat. Prick the sausage in several places with a fork, add to the pan, and cook until it begins to render its fat, 1 to 2 minutes. Add the chicken and cook, turning, until browned on all sides, 6 to 7 minutes. Remove the sausage and chicken from the pan and set aside.

2 Add the vinegar to the pot and stir up the browned bits from the bottom of the pan. Cook until most of the vinegar has evaporated, about 1 minute, and then add the onion and peppers. Increase the heat to high and cook, stirring constantly, until the peppers begin to soften, 3 to 4 minutes. Stir in the rice, then the tomatoes with their juices, the chicken stock, chicken, sausage, basil, oregano, and hot pepper to taste.

3 Cover and simmer gently, stirring occasionally, until the chicken is tender and no longer pink in the center and the rice is tender, about 40 minutes. If the rice seems too dry toward the end of cooking, add a small amount of water to moisten. Season with salt to taste.

White Bean, Chicken & Sausage Cassoulet

Instead of starting with a whole chicken, this can be made with chicken necks, backs, and carcasses, if you have them on hand.

MAKES:
6 to 8 servings

SOAK:
12 hours or overnight

PREP:
25 minutes

COOK:
1 hour, 10 minutes

1 In a large soup pot, combine the beans, chicken, the quartered onion, the celery, carrot, whole garlic clove, the bay leaves, allspice berries, 4 cups water, salt, and hot red pepper. Cover and bring to a boil. Reduce the heat to medium-low and simmer gently until the beans are tender, about 1½ hours, stirring periodically and adding more water if the mixture becomes too dry.

2 Remove the vegetables and the chicken; discard the vegetables. When the chicken is cool enough to handle, remove the meat from the bones in large pieces. Return the chicken meat to the pot along with the sausage, tomatoes, diced onion, and minced garlic. Cook, uncovered, over medium heat for 10 minutes. Remove and discard the bay leaves. Stir in the sage, basil, vinegar, pepper, and additional salt, if needed.

12	ounces dried navy or Great Northern beans, soaked 12 hours or overnight
1	small frying chicken (about 3 pounds), cut into serving pieces and skin removed
2	large onions, 1 quartered and 1 diced
1	celery rib, cut into chunks
1	medium carrot, peeled and cut into chunks
3	large garlic cloves, 1 whole and 2 minced
3	bay leaves
3	whole allspice berries
1½	teaspoons salt
¼	teaspoon crushed hot red pepper

2	smoked garlic-spiced sausages, such as Kielbasa, cut into 1-inch pieces
2	tomatoes, diced

2	tablespoons minced fresh sage
2	tablespoons minced fresh basil
1	tablespoon wine vinegar
1	teaspoon coarsely ground pepper

Colombian Chicken, Potato & Avocado Stew

Called ajiaco *in Colombia, traditional renderings of this stew stand as a testament to potatoes, which are native to the region. There, as many as 10 varieties of potatoes are used in the stew, from tiny waxy ones to those that are big and mealy. Here, as many types can be used as are available. Yukon golds, reds, russets, and sweet potatoes are a good basic group to which others can be added, including the Peruvian purple potato.*

MAKES:
4 to 6 servings
PREP:
35 minutes
COOK:
55 minutes

4½ cups chicken stock or reduced-sodium canned broth

3 medium red potatoes, scrubbed and cut into chunks

3 medium yellow potatoes, scrubbed and cut into chunks

1 medium sweet potato, scrubbed and cut into chunks

1 medium russet potato, scrubbed and cut into chunks

1 large onion, cut into thin wedges

⅓ pound ready-cut baby carrots

1 small dried hot red pepper

2 bay leaves

1 teaspoon coarsely ground black pepper

½ teaspoon ground coriander

6 to 8 cilantro stems plus ¼ cup minced cilantro leaves

1 cooked (3-pound) chicken, skinned, meat torn into large pieces

2 small ears of corn, shucked and cut into 4 pieces each

3 scallions, sliced

⅓ cup heavy cream

½ teaspoon salt

1 avocado, peeled and diced

1½ tablespoons drained capers

1 In a large saucepan, combine the chicken stock, potatoes, onion, carrots, hot pepper, bay leaves, black pepper, coriander, and cilantro stems. Bring to a boil, cover, and simmer until the potatoes are almost tender, about 35 minutes. Add the chicken and corn. Cook, uncovered, until the potatoes and corn are tender, about 20 minutes.

2 Stir in the scallions, cream, salt, and minced cilantro leaves. Divide the stew between serving bowls and serve topped with the avocado and capers.

Although they look alike and people frequently confuse their names, yams and **sweet potatoes** are not even distantly related. They come from two entirely different botanical families. Yams are actually related to grasses and lilies, and sweet potatoes aren't even related to the common potato species.

There are two broad types of sweet potatoes. One has pale yellow meat with a dry flesh and the other has dark orange meat with a moist flesh. Dark orange sweet potatoes are plumper and slightly sweeter than the yellow variety. Pick sweet potatoes with firm, smooth skins.

Capers are the small, very salty, pickled flower buds of a Mediterranean bush. They are used whole as a piquant flavoring or garnish. The tiny variety called *nonpareil* is generally considered the finest. You can rinse capers before using to remove excess salt if desired.

Chicken Pot au Feu

New Englanders have boiled dinners, Chinese the fire pot, and French the pot au feu. All are variations on meat and vegetables boiled together in a flavored broth. Chicken adapts to the method very nicely, especially when some boldly seasoned sausages are added to the mix. Don't feel confined to only the vegetables listed here. Many others work just as well.

MAKES:
4 servings

PREP:
20 minutes

COOK:
45 minutes

1½ tablespoons olive oil

4 smoked sausages, preferably a spiced chicken or turkey sausage

4 chicken thighs or breasts

1 large onion, diced

5 cups chicken stock or reduced-sodium canned broth

1 pound Savoy or green cabbage, cut into 4 wedges

6 small red potatoes, cut in half

4 large carrots, peeled and cut into thirds

2 medium yellow summer squash, cut into 1-inch lengths

4 very small turnips, peeled

2 bay leaves

2 parsley sprigs

1 strip of lemon rind, about 2 inches long

½ teaspoon salt
Freshly ground pepper

Minced fresh tarragon or parsley

1 In a large soup pot, heat the oil over medium-high heat. Add the sausages and cook, turning occasionally, until they are browned on all sides, 5 to 6 minutes. Set the sausage aside. Add the chicken and cook, turning once or twice, until browned on both sides, 6 to 8 minutes. Set aside the chicken with the sausages.

2 Add the onion to the same pan and cook over medium heat, stirring constantly, just until the onion begins to soften, 4 to 5 minutes. (Do not let it brown.)

3 Return the chicken to the pot. Add the chicken stock, cabbage, potatoes, carrots, squash, turnips, bay leaves, parsley sprigs, and lemon rind. Bring to a boil. Cover, reduce the heat to medium-low, and simmer 15 minutes. Add the sausages and simmer gently until the turnips and potatoes are tender, 10 to 15 minutes longer. Season with the salt and pepper to taste.

4 To serve, transfer the chicken, sausages, and vegetables to a large tureen or serving platter with a slotted spoon. Sprinkle with the tarragon. Skim the fat from the broth and remove and discard the bay leaves, parsley, and lemon rind. Add the broth to the tureen or, if serving on a platter, moisten the meat and vegetables with the broth, and pass the remainder separately.

Turkey Breast with Stewed Barley & Leek Pilaf

Simple and sturdy are apt descriptions of this stovetop preparation. But, above all, the dish is loaded with a charm that makes it appropriate for all kinds of meals, from family feasts to cozy dinners with friends.

MAKES: 6 servings
PREP: 15 minutes
COOK: 1 hour, 15 minutes

1 In a large, deep-sided sauté pan or Dutch oven, cook the bacon over medium heat until it is crisp, about 5 minutes. Remove the bacon with a slotted spoon, and set aside. Add the turkey breast to the pan and season with salt and pepper. Cook, turning, until well browned on both sides, 10 to 12 minutes. Remove the turkey to a plate. Add the leeks and cook, stirring often, until they are tender, 5 to 6 minutes. Season with about ¼ teaspoon salt and the desired amount of pepper.

2 Add the barley to the pan along with 2¾ cups of the chicken stock, the garlic, carrots, bay leaves, and thyme. Place the turkey on top, skin-side up. Bring to a boil, cover, and reduce the heat to medium-low. Simmer gently, turning the turkey once after 30 minutes, until the barley is tender and the turkey is white throughout, 50 to 60 minutes. If the barley seems too dry, add the remaining ¼ cup chicken stock. Set the turkey aside and tent with foil.

2	bacon slices, diced
1	bone-in turkey breast half (about 3 pounds) **Salt and freshly ground pepper**
3	medium leeks, cleaned, trimmed, and sliced ½ inch thick
¾	cup pearl barley
3	cups chicken stock or reduced-sodium canned broth or water
2	medium garlic cloves, minced
2	medium carrots, peeled and diced
3	bay leaves
1	teaspoon dried thyme leaves
¼	cup heavy cream

3 Add the cream, bacon, and ½ teaspoon pepper to the barley and boil until the mixture is creamy, 4 to 5 minutes. Remove and discard the bay leaves. Gently stir in the leeks and remove the pan from the heat. Season with salt to taste.

4 To serve, spread the barley mixture on a platter. Remove and discard the skin from the turkey and slice the meat. Arrange the meat in overlapping slices over the barley.

Vegetable Stew with Turkey Meatballs

Meatballs seem to have been left behind in the pursuit of new tastes and new trends. But a gentle reminder every now and then proves that they deserve a continuing spot in the repertoire of the table. Turkey is a lower-fat alternative to beef, and it works very well here, in a light, stovetop stew that is finished with a bounty of vegetables. With spicing that is vaguely suggestive of Tex-Mex tastes, there's no reason not to add a garnish of diced avocado, shredded cheese, and cilantro to each serving.

MAKES:
3 to 4 servings

PREP:
15 minutes

COOK:
45 minutes

1	slice of soft white bread
3	tablespoons milk

3	tablespoons finely minced onion
1	pound ground turkey
2	teaspoons chili powder
½	teaspoon ground cumin
½	teaspoon salt
½	teaspoon freshly ground pepper

1½	tablespoons vegetable oil

1	cup chicken stock or reduced-sodium canned broth
3	tablespoons flour

1	(14½-ounce) can diced tomatoes, juices reserved
2	large carrots, peeled and halved crosswise, then quartered lengthwise
2	celery ribs, each rib cut diagonally in half
1	slender zucchini, halved crosswise, then quartered lengthwise
1	ear of corn, shucked and cut crosswise into four pieces

1 In a medium bowl, place the bread and milk. Let stand 10 minutes, and then stir until the bread dissolves into a paste. Add the onion, turkey, 1 teaspoon of the chili powder, ¼ teaspoon of the cumin, the salt, and pepper. Mix with your hands until well blended and shape into eight meatballs.

2 In a large saucepan, heat the oil on medium-high heat. Add the meatballs and cook, turning occasionally, until browned, about 10 minutes. Remove to a plate.

3 In a small bowl, blend ⅓ cup of the chicken stock with the flour to make a smooth paste. Add the flour paste to the saucepan along with the remaining chicken stock, 1 teaspoon chili powder, ¼ teaspoon cumin, the tomatoes with their juices, and the vegetables. Bring to a boil. Reduce the heat to medium-low, cover, and simmer gently until the vegetables are almost tender, about 15 minutes. Add the meatballs and continue cooking until the vegetables are tender, 5 to 8 minutes.

Chili powder is a commercial spice blend of chili peppers, cumin seed, garlic, oregano, salt, and sometimes cloves or allspice. Although it's typically associated with chili, you also can use it to season meats, poultry, and seafood. Try creating your own special chili powder blend from the seasonings listed above.

To make sure your meatballs are similar in size so they cook evenly, try the following trick: on a piece of waxed paper, pat the ground meat mixture into a square. Divide the meat into the number of meatballs needed by cutting it into smaller squares, and then roll each square into a ball.

Generous steaks, thick-cut pork chops, and gorgeous roasts have long reflected abundance, and they continue to be a large part of culinary expression. In the not-so-distant past, we may have wavered a bit in our affection for meat—or at least we said we did. Concerns about health seemed to cast red meat in a bad light. But with moderation and balance serving as sensible guiding hands, meat is back in a big way. Once again, it is taking its rightful and well-earned place at the meal table, bringing with it the same sense of bounty and well-being that it once held.

There's no reason for meaty meals to be marked by tedium. With so many different cuts, from lean flank steaks to meaty shanks and short ribs, succulent oxtails and richly flavored round steak, ground meat to boldly flavored sausages, meals can be varied in form and style. **Shanghai Short Ribs**, **Cuban Salmagundi**, **Osso Bucco**, and **Lamb Stew with Orzo** bring global tastes to the gourmet table. Many of the meats are paired with vegetables or beans, clever ways of offering a more healthy and favorable ratio of protein to carbohydrates. **Braised Round Steak with Country Garden Vegetables**, **Beef Stew with the Right Attitude**, **Green Chili Pork Stew**, and **Hip Hoppin' John** are but a few of the offerings that show how meat evolves and keeps pace with changing diets and taste preferences.

Meaty Dinners

Cooking styles are varied for meats, carefully designed to flatter the cut. Ground meats, used in the **Persian Rice Cake with Lamb & Spinach** and the African-inspired **Bobotie**, cook quickly and without a lot of fuss. Other, tougher meats, such as shanks, oxtails, and pot roasts, require long, slow cooking before their finest assets and full flavors are brought to the fore. These meats tend to have a higher fat content. However, if the dish is carefully skimmed before serving, much of the fat can be discarded, so the final effect is leaner. The gloriously rich flavor, however, remains fully intact.

Flemish Beef & Beer Stew

The affinity for onions, beef, and beer is on tap in this rich, autumn-into-winter stew. The onions, offered in equal parts to the beef, are cooked until their natural sugars caramelize. This is met head-on by the addition of beer, which tames the sweetness with its own appealingly bitter edge.

MAKES:
6 servings
PREP:
15 minutes
COOK:
2 hours, 15 minutes

1 In a large flameproof casserole, cook the bacon over medium heat, turning occasionally, until it is crisp, about 5 minutes. With a slotted spoon, transfer the bacon to paper towels and set aside. Add the onions to the drippings in the pan, and cook over medium-low heat until the onions are very soft, about 20 minutes. Sprinkle on the brown sugar, increase the heat to medium-high, and cook, stirring often, until the onions turn a rich golden brown, about 8 minutes. Add the vinegar, salt, and pepper. Transfer to a bowl.

2 Preheat the oven to 350° F. Heat the oil in the casserole. Add the meat in batches and cook, turning occasionally, until the meat is browned on all sides, 6 to 8 minutes per batch. Return the meat to the casserole, sprinkle on the flour, and stir well. Cook, stirring constantly, 1 minute. Add the beer, thyme, onions, and bacon, and remove from the heat.

3 Cover the casserole and transfer to the oven. Bake about 1½ hours, or until the meat is tender.

3	bacon slices, preferably applewood-smoked, diced
3 to 4	large onions, halved crosswise and cut into ½-inch wedges
2	teaspoons brown sugar
1	tablespoon cider vinegar
¾	teaspoon salt
¼	teaspoon freshly ground pepper
1	tablespoon vegetable oil
2	pounds lean beef stew meat, cut into 1-inch cubes and patted dry
3	tablespoons flour
1	(12-ounce) bottle dark beer
½	teaspoon dried thyme leaves

Mexican-Style Rolled Flank Steak

Well before the global penchant for Mexican food took off, flank steak, stuffed with cornbread and quietly spiced with cumin and cayenne pepper, showed up in cookbooks. Its popularity endures, and this time it is updated with the smoky taste of chipotle chiles and the lusty edge of beer.

MAKES:
4 servings

PREP:
10 minutes

COOK:
1 hour,
20 minutes

STAND:
5 to 10 minutes

1 medium onion

2 to 3 tablespoons chipotle chilies in adobo sauce

2 tablespoons vegetable oil

1 medium garlic clove, minced

1 poblano or small green bell pepper, finely diced

1 serrano pepper, seeded and minced

1/2 teaspoon ground cumin

1 1/2 cups packaged cornbread stuffing mix

1 egg, lightly beaten

1/2 cup chicken stock or reduced-sodium canned broth

1 small flank steak (about 1 1/4 pounds)

1/4 teaspoon salt

1 1/4 cups beer

1 1/4 cups diced fresh tomatoes or 1 (14 1/2-ounce) can diced tomatoes, drained

1 tablespoon tomato paste

1 tablespoon brown sugar

1 Cut the onion into ½-inch wedges. Reserve half of the wedges for later use and chop the remaining wedges. In a small bowl, smash the chipotle chilies with the back of a spoon to make a coarse paste, and set aside.

2 In a large sauté pan that is at least 3 inches deep or a saucepan, heat 1 tablespoon of the oil over medium heat. Add the chopped onion, garlic, poblano and serrano peppers, and cumin and cook, stirring occasionally, until the peppers are softened, 5 to 6 minutes. Add the cornbread stuffing mix and cook 1 minute. Transfer to a medium bowl and cool slightly. Add the egg and the chicken stock and mix well.

3 Rub one side of the flank steak with about 1 tablespoon of the chipotle paste and season with the salt. Spread the cornbread mixture over the paste, packing it into an even layer. Starting at a short end, roll up the steak jelly-roll fashion and secure in two places with heavy string.

4 Heat the remaining 1 tablespoon oil in the same pan. Add the meat and cook, turning occasionally, until browned all over, 10 to 12 minutes. Add the onion wedges, beer, tomatoes, tomato paste, brown sugar, and additional chipotle chili paste to taste.

5 Cover and bring to a boil. Reduce the heat to medium-low and simmer gently until the meat is tender, 50 to 60 minutes, adding more liquid if the meat seems too dry. Let stand 5 to 10 minutes before slicing.

Chipotle chilies are smoke-dried, ripened jalapeño chilies. They often come canned in thick **adobo sauce**, a dark red tangy paste or sauce of Mexican origin whose basic ingredients include vinegar, soy sauce, herbs, and chilies. Adobo sauce is used both as a marinade and as a serving sauce.

Serrano chili peppers are almost as spicy as jalapeños. They measure about the same length, but are more slender, with a diameter of about ½ inch. They're sold green, ripened red, and pickled in brine.

Braised Round Steak with Country Garden Vegetables

MAKES:
4 servings

PREP:
20 minutes

COOK:
1 hour,
10 minutes

Generations have grown up on dishes like this slow-simmered round steak surrounded with a collection of vegetables that is decided as much by the cook's whimsy as it is by any strict formula.

2	tablespoons flour
½	teaspoon ground cumin
½	teaspoon salt
½	teaspoon freshly ground pepper
1½	pounds top round steak
2	tablespoons olive oil
1	medium onion, diced
1	(14½-ounce) can diced tomatoes, juices reserved
2	large celery ribs, diagonally cut into 1-inch lengths
2	small ears of corn, shucked and cut crosswise into 4 pieces each
2	small zucchini, halved lengthwise, then cut crosswise into 1-inch lengths
3	scallions
½	cup cilantro or parsley leaves
1	fresh jalapeño or serrano pepper, seeded and minced

1 In a large plastic food storage bag, combine the flour, cumin, salt, and pepper. Add the meat, close the bag tightly, and shake to coat the meat evenly with the flour mixture.

2 In a 12-inch nonreactive sauté pan or large saucepan, heat the olive oil over medium-high heat. Add the meat and cook, turning, until browned on both sides, 10 to 12 minutes. Add the onion and the tomatoes with their juices. Cover, reduce the heat to low, and cook gently 35 minutes.

3 Add the celery and corn and cook until the meat is almost tender, 20 minutes longer. Add the zucchini, pressing it into the pan juices. Cover and cook until all the vegetables and the meat are tender, 5 to 10 minutes longer.

4 Mince together the scallions, cilantro, and jalapeño pepper. Sprinkle over the meat and vegetables just before serving.

Asian Oxtails

With their sturdy character, oxtails are normally partnered with root vegetables, a tomato sauce, and perhaps a handful of barley. It's a grand treatment, but there are other avenues to explore, here, a delicate Asian theme. The vegetables, added after the oxtails have been simmered to delectable submission, remain fresh and bright green, a vivid contrast to the meltingly tender meat.

MAKES:
3 to 4 servings

PREP:
15 minutes

COOK:
2 hours, 50 minutes

REFRIGERATE:
several hours

REHEAT:
10 minutes

1 In a large pot, heat the peanut and sesame oils over high heat. Add the oxtails in batches and cook, turning occasionally, until browned on all sides, 8 to 10 minutes. Add the sherry and vinegar and cook 30 seconds. Add the chicken stock, four slices of the ginger, and the soy sauce; cover and bring to a boil.

2 Reduce the heat to medium-low and simmer gently until the oxtails are tender, 2½ to 3 hours, or longer if needed. Remove from the heat and cool slightly. Refrigerate until the fat solidifies. Skim all fat from the surface and remove and discard the ginger.

3 Return the pan to medium-heat and bring to a boil. Cook 5 minutes. Add the bok choy, snow peas, scallions, and hot red pepper, and cook, stirring often, until the vegetables are crisp-tender, 4 to 5 minutes. Mince the remaining 2 slices of ginger and stir them into the broth. Season with additional soy sauce, if desired.

1½   tablespoons peanut oil

1½   teaspoons Asian sesame oil

4   pounds oxtails, cut into pieces

¼   cup dry sherry

¼   cup seasoned rice vinegar

4   cups chicken stock or reduced-sodium canned broth

6   thin slices of fresh ginger

1   tablespoon soy sauce

1   small head of bok choy, cut into 1-inch slices

⅓   pound snow peas, trimmed

4   scallions, diagonally cut into 1-inch lengths

Pinch of crushed hot red pepper

Mediterranean Beef Stew with Olives & Prunes

Provençal French influences abound in this hearty and aromatic stew. As with all stews, this one is even better and more complex when it's reheated, so plan on making it ahead. Creamy polenta with mascarpone cheese is an indulgent and utterly delightful side dish.

MAKES
4 to 6 servings

MARINADE:
1 hour to 1 week

PREP:
20 minutes

COOK:
2 hours, 25 minutes

¾ cup pitted prunes

½ cup port wine

¼ cup olive oil

3 medium onions, cut into 1-inch dice

½ teaspoon salt

1 tablespoon wine vinegar

2 medium garlic cloves, sliced paper-thin

1 teaspoon grated orange zest

½ teaspoon dried thyme leaves

2 pounds beef stew meat, cut into 1-inch cubes

1½ teaspoons ground coriander

2 tablespoons flour

3 celery ribs, cut into 1-inch lengths

1 (14½-ounce) can beef broth

⅔ cup green olives

Freshly ground pepper

1 In a small plastic food storage bag, combine the prunes and port and let stand at least 1 hour while you begin the stew or for as long as a week.

2 In a large flameproof casserole, heat 1½ tablespoons of the olive oil over high heat. Add the onions and ¼ teaspoon of the salt. Cook, stirring often, until the onions begin to brown at the edges, about 4 minutes. Reduce the heat to low and cook until the onions are soft, 8 minutes longer.

3 Add the vinegar, garlic, orange zest, thyme, and 1 tablespoon of the port drained from the prunes, and cook 1 minute. Transfer the onions to a small bowl and set aside.

4 Preheat the oven to 350° F. Season the meat with the remaining ¼ teaspoon salt and the coriander. Heat the remaining 2½ tablespoons of oil in the casserole. Add the meat in batches and cook, turning occasionally, until the meat is browned on all sides, 6 to 8 minutes per batch. Return the meat to the casserole, sprinkle on the flour, and mix well. Add the celery and beef broth and heat to a simmer.

5 Remove the casserole from the heat and cover tightly. Transfer to the oven and bake 1½ hours. Add the olives, onions, prunes, and any remaining port that hasn't been absorbed. Bake until the meat is tender, 30 to 45 minutes longer. Season with additional salt and pepper to taste.

Prunes are a variety of dried plum. They come in many sizes, and their rich-tasting, dark, fairly moist flesh makes them perfect for eating out of hand, or as an ingredient in sweet and savory dishes and in baking.

The best **stew meats** are inexpensive cuts with plenty of collagen, or connective tissue, such as beef chuck, lamb shoulder, pork shoulder, and veal shoulder or breast. The slow process of wet cooking softens the collagen, producing fork-tender bites of meat.

Ceylonese-Spiced Beef Stew

A judicious amount of hot chili pepper serves as just the right counterpoint to the aromatic spices that lie at the heart of this stew. Serve it with Indian flatbread, such as nan or chapati, and a cooling salad of cucumbers in yogurt sauce.

MAKES:
4 to 6 servings

PREP:
25 minutes

COOK:
1 hour,
20 minutes

2 tablespoons vegetable oil

1½ pounds lean beef stew meat, cut into 1-inch cubes, patted dry

¼ teaspoon salt

¼ teaspoon cayenne

1 large onion, diced

1 large garlic clove, minced

1 jalapeño or serrano pepper, minced

1 piece of fresh ginger (about a 1-inch cube), minced

1 teaspoon ground cumin

1 teaspoon ground coriander

1 teaspoon ground turmeric

⅛ teaspoon cinnamon

1 (14½-ounce) can diced tomatoes, juices reserved

2 medium red potatoes, scrubbed and cut into 1-inch cubes

1 cup cauliflower florets

1 cup tiny frozen peas, thawed

¼ cup minced fresh mint

1 Preheat the oven to 350° F. In a flameproof Dutch oven, heat 1 tablespoon of the oil over high heat. Sprinkle the meat with a small amount of the salt and cayenne. Add the meat to the pan in batches and cook, turning occasionally, until browned on all sides, 6 to 8 minutes per batch. Remove the meat from the pan and set aside.

2 Heat the remaining 1 tablespoon oil in the same pan. Add the onion and cook over high heat, stirring often, until it is softened and golden, about 5 minutes. Add the garlic, jalapeño pepper, and ginger and cook, stirring constantly, for 1 minute. Add the cumin, coriander, turmeric, cinnamon, and the remaining salt and cayenne. Cook and stir 20 seconds. Add the tomatoes with their juices, 1¼ cups water, and the meat. Cover tightly, transfer to the oven, and bake 30 minutes.

3 Add the potatoes and cauliflower. Cover and bake until the meat and potatoes are tender, about 1 hour. Stir in the peas and mint.

Bobotie

By tradition, this is considered an African dish, but many influences, especially English and Indian, are evident. It's a richly flavored offering, with lamb generously spiced, then sweetened with dried fruits and a hint of mango chutney. The custard topping, here made with coconut milk, is silky and light, a fine balance to the meat mixture.

MAKES:
6 to 8 servings

PREP:
10 minutes

COOK:
50 minutes

STAND:
10 minutes

1 | Preheat the oven to 350° F. In a large flameproof casserole, melt the butter over medium-high heat. Add the onion, garlic, ginger, and jalapeño pepper and cook, stirring often, until the onion begins to soften, about 5 minutes.

2 | Stir in the curry powder and cook 1 minute. Add the lamb and cook, stirring often, until it is well browned, 8 to 10 minutes. Stir in the apricots, currants, apple, chutney, tamarind paste, and ½ teaspoon salt. Cook, stirring often, until the bottom of the skillet is almost dry, 5 to 6 minutes.

3 | In a medium bowl, whisk the eggs to blend. Whisk in the coconut milk, milk, and a pinch each of salt and cayenne. Pour over the lamb mixture. Bake 40 minutes, or until the custard is lightly set. Let stand 10 minutes before serving.

1   **tablespoon unsalted butter**

1   **medium onion, minced**

1   **garlic clove, minced**

1   **medium piece of fresh ginger (about a ½-inch cube), minced**

1   **small jalapeño or serrano pepper, seeded and minced**

2   **tablespoons curry powder**

2   **pounds ground lamb**

⅓   **cup minced dried apricots**

¼   **cup currants or raisins**

1   **small tart apple, chopped**

2   **tablespoons mango chutney**

1   **teaspoon tamarind paste or 1 tablespoon fresh lemon juice**

½   **teaspoon salt plus a large pinch more**

3   **eggs**

¾   **cup unsweetened coconut milk**

¾   **cup milk**

    Pinch of cayenne

Beef Stew with the Right Attitude

In the 1930s and 1940s, long before such a lifestyle was considered stylish, Haydn Pearson wrote what were described as inspirational pieces on country life. In one, he wrote a narrative on beef stew, expressing perturbation over its decline. A great champion of the dish he called humble, he listed as the first requirement the right attitude, an attitude of leisure and concentration. He then noted the ingredients he felt were important, and those are the basis for this stew.

MAKES:
6 to 8 servings
PREP:
30 minutes
COOK:
1 hour,
45 minutes

2½ tablespoons olive oil

2 pounds beef stew meat, cut into ¾-inch cubes and patted dry

2 tablespoons flour

2 large onions, diced

1 tablespoon red wine vinegar

1 cup dry red wine

1 cup beef stock or reduced-sodium canned broth

2 tablespoons tomato paste

3 small yellow or red potatoes, scrubbed and cut into chunks

2 medium sweet potatoes, peeled and cut into chunks

3 large carrots, peeled and sliced

2 large celery ribs, sliced

1 medium turnip, peeled and diced

1 small wedge of green cabbage, chopped (about 1½ cups)

1 teaspoon dried basil

½ teaspoon crumbled dried rosemary

¼ cup minced parsley

1 teaspoon salt

Freshly ground pepper

1 Preheat the oven to 325° F. In a large flameproof casserole, heat 1 tablespoon of the olive oil over high heat. Add half of the meat and cook, turning occasionally, until browned on all sides, 6 to 8 minutes. Toss with half the flour; remove from the pan. Repeat with another ½ tablespoon of olive oil and the remaining meat and flour.

2 Heat the remaining 1 tablespoon of olive oil in the same casserole. Add the onions and cook, stirring often, until they begin to soften, 3 to 4 minutes. Add the vinegar and 2 tablespoons of the wine and stir up the browned bits from the bottom of the pan. Remove from the heat. Add the remaining wine, the beef stock, tomato paste, vegetables, herbs, and meat, and stir well.

3 Cover and transfer to the oven. Bake until the meat and potatoes are tender, about 1½ hours. Stir in the parsley, salt, and pepper to taste.

Port is a sweet fortified wine most often served after meals. Grape alcohol is added to the wine partway through fermentation, which stops the process at a point where the wine has plenty of sweetness and a higher alcohol content. Port wines originated in the Douro Valley in Northern Portugal; the best ports still come from that area. Wines shipped out of the Portuguese city of Oporto are labeled Porto, rather than port.

Because of the many types of port, the various labels can be confusing. The best and most expensive are vintage ports. Late-bottled vintage ports and single vintage ports are also made from grapes of a single vintage, although the grapes are of lower quality than those for vintage ports. Tawny ports are a blend of grapes from several different years. Vintage character ports are essentially high-quality ruby ports, which are considered the lowest grade of port. They're blended from several vintages and are the lightest and fruitiest in flavor.

Green Chili Pork Stew

There are many versions of this classic stew, most of them proffering meltingly tender chunks of pork, simmered with a variety of green chili peppers that add varying degrees of heat along with their herbaceous taste. This one reaches just the right balance. If you can get rendered lard, be sure to use it for the wonderfully authentic dimension it adds to the stew.

MAKES:
6 servings

PREP:
20 minutes

COOK:
1 hour,
35 minutes

3	tablespoons flour
1	teaspoon ground cumin
1	teaspoon rubbed sage
1	teaspoon salt
2	pounds pork stew meat, cut into 1-inch cubes

3	tablespoons rendered lard or vegetable oil

2	large onions, chopped
3	tablespoons cider vinegar

6	small red potatoes, quartered
1	poblano pepper, diced
2	Anaheims or other mild green chili peppers, diced
10	tomatillos, chopped
1½	cups chicken stock or reduced-sodium canned broth
1	teaspoon brown sugar

½	cup chopped cilantro

1 In a large plastic food storage bag, combine the flour, cumin, sage, and salt. Add the meat, seal the bag, and shake well to coat the meat evenly. In a large, heavy pot, heat the lard over high heat. Add the meat in batches and cook, turning occasionally, until the meat is browned on all sides, 6 to 8 minutes per batch. Remove to a plate as it browns.

2 Add the onions to the pan and reduce the heat to medium. Pour the vinegar over the onions and scrape up the browned bits of flour from the bottom of the pan. Simmer, stirring occasionally, 5 minutes.

3 Add the potatoes, poblano pepper, chili peppers, tomatillos, chicken stock, brown sugar, and pork. Reduce the heat to medium-low, cover, and simmer gently until the meat is tender, 1¼ hours. Stir in the cilantro just before serving.

Red Curry Pork & Sweet Potato Stew

Ready-made curry pastes, carefully blended from long lists of complex ingredients, are a staple throughout Thailand. Increasingly, supermarkets stock curry pastes, from tamer yellow to powerfully potent green and red. They provide a simple way to add a big taste to many dishes, including this exotic stew.

MAKES:
4 servings
PREP:
20 minutes
COOK:
1 hour,
50 minutes

1 Preheat the oven to 350° F. In a large flameproof casserole, heat the oil over high heat. Add the pork, in batches if necessary, and cook, turning, until browned on all sides, 6 to 8 minutes per batch. With a slotted spoon, remove the meat from the pan. Add the onion and lemongrass to the pan and cook, stirring often, until the onion begins to brown at the edges, about 3 minutes. Add the sweet potatoes, chicken stock, curry paste, and pork.

2 Cover the casserole and transfer to the oven. Bake 1½ hours, or until the pork and sweet potatoes are tender. In a small bowl, blend the flour with 2 tablespoons cold water to form a paste. Stir into the stew. Bring to a boil on top of the stove and cook, stirring, until the juices thicken, about 2 minutes. Sprinkle the peanuts and cilantro on top before serving.

1	tablespoon vegetable oil
1½	pounds pork stew meat, cut into 1-inch cubes
1	large onion, cut into ½-inch wedges
1	large stalk of lemongrass, trimmed and minced
2	medium sweet potatoes, cut into 1½-inch chunks
2	cups chicken stock or reduced-sodium canned broth
2 to 3	teaspoons red curry paste
2	tablespoons flour
3	tablespoons chopped peanuts
3	tablespoons minced cilantro

Shanghai Short Ribs

Cuts of meat that snuggle against bones, such as short ribs, are among the richest and most flavorful. That luxury comes with a price, though. They require hours of cooking for their greatest potential to develop. But with the benefit of simple, unattended cooking, the recalcitrant meat turns meltingly tender.

MAKES:
2 to 3 servings

PREP:
15 minutes

COOK:
1 hour, 50 minutes

REFRIGERATE:
overnight (optional)

ADDITIONAL COOKING:
30 minutes

1½ tablespoons Asian sesame oil

3 pounds beef short ribs

1 small onion, chopped

1 large garlic clove, minced

1 large piece of fresh ginger
(about a 1½-inch cube), minced

⅓ cup dry sherry

⅓ cup seasoned rice vinegar

2 cups beef stock or reduced-sodium
canned broth

¼ cup hoisin sauce

2 tablespoons soy sauce

1 teaspoon Asian chili paste, or more to taste

3 carrots, peeled and diagonally cut into
½-inch lengths

2 celery ribs, diagonally cut into ½-inch lengths

3 scallions, diagonally cut into ½-inch lengths

2 tablespoons toasted sesame seeds

1 In a large, heavy pot, heat the oil over high heat. Add the ribs in batches and cook, turning, until browned, 8 to 10 minutes per batch. Stir in the onion, garlic, and ginger and cook, stirring, 2 minutes. Add the sherry and vinegar; stir up the browned bits from the bottom of the pan. Boil 2 minutes.

2 Add the beef stock, hoisin sauce, soy sauce, and chili paste, cover, and bring to a boil. Reduce the heat to medium-low and simmer gently until the ribs are almost tender, about 1½ hours. Skim the fat from the surface or refrigerate overnight until the fat solidifies, so it can be removed. Reheat before finishing.

3 Add the carrots and celery to the pot and cook, uncovered, until the vegetables and meat are tender, 30 to 40 minutes. Sprinkle with the scallions and sesame seeds just before serving.

Also called Peking sauce, **hoisin sauce** is a thick, sweet, and spicy reddish-brown liquid widely used in Chinese cooking. This fermented mixture combines soybeans or wheat, garlic, chili peppers, vinegar, sesame seeds, and various spices. Hoisin sauce is mainly used as a table condiment and as a flavoring agent for many meat, poultry, and shellfish dishes. You'll find it in large supermarkets and in Asian grocery stores.

Sesame seeds are tiny, ivory-colored seeds with a mild, nutty flavor. They're also available in black. Both types are used most often as a garnish on sweet and savory dishes. The sesame seed is the first recorded seasoning, dating back to 3,000 B.C., in Assyria. Much later, African slaves brought the seeds to America. They called them *benné* (pronounced BEHN-nee) seeds, and they became very popular in Southern cooking. You can buy the seeds packaged in supermarkets, or in bulk at Middle Eastern markets and health-food stores.

To toast sesame seeds, place them in a small, dry, heavy frying pan over moderate heat and stir until they are aromatic, 1 to 2 minutes. Cool slightly before using.

Hip Hoppin' John

Hoppin' John has a long history in the Southern United States, most notably as an integral part of the New Year's Day celebration. No matter when it graces the table, it's a felicitous mixture of beans and rice, simmered into a rich amalgam of flavors. Here, it's a little more jazzed up than tradition dictates, with some colorful vegetables added at the end so they stay vibrant and fresh. Be sure to serve lots of cornbread and maybe a mess of greens on the side.

MAKES:
8 to 10 servings

PREP:
15 minutes

COOK:
2 hours,
20 minutes

1   **pound dried black-eyed peas**

2   **smoked ham hocks**

2   **medium onions**

3   **large garlic cloves**

2   **bay leaves**

1   **cup converted long-grain white rice**

1   **(10-ounce) can diced tomatoes with chili peppers, juices reserved**

1   **large red bell pepper, finely diced**

3   **large celery ribs, diced**

1   **fresh jalapeño or serrano pepper, minced**

2   **teaspoons Creole seasoning blend**

¾   **teaspoon dried thyme leaves**

¾   **teaspoon ground cumin**

¾   **teaspoon salt**

3   **scallions, sliced**

    Hot red pepper sauce

1   In a large pot, combine the black-eyed peas, ham hocks, and 6 cups water. Cut 1 onion in half and add it to the pot along with the garlic and bay leaves. Bring to a boil, reduce the heat to medium-low, and simmer gently until the beans are tender but not mushy, 2 to 2½ hours. Remove the hocks, cut off the meat in large shreds, and set the meat aside. Drain the peas and set aside. Remove and discard the bay leaves, onion, and garlic.

2   Add 2½ cups of water to the pot and bring to a boil. Add the rice, cover, and simmer until the rice is almost tender, 12 minutes.

3   Mince the remaining onion. Add it to the rice along with the peas, tomatoes with their juices, bell pepper, celery, jalapeño pepper, Creole seasoning, thyme, cumin, and salt. Cook until the rice is tender, 5 to 7 minutes. Stir in the sliced scallions and meat from the ham hocks. Pass the hot sauce at the table.

Eggplant & Sausage Stew

Abundantly filled with vegetables, this earthy meal-in-a-bowl straddles the line between soup and stew. From its fragrant aroma to hearty sustenance, it offers the best of both. Paired with a simple green salad with a mustard dressing and lots of bread, it's ideal for casual, unfussy meals.

MAKES:
6 servings

PREP:
20 minutes

COOK:
1 hour, 10 minutes

1 In a large pot, heat the olive oil over medium-high heat. Add the onion, garlic, and chile pepper. Cook, stirring occasionally, until the onion begins to soften, 4 to 5 minutes. Add the fennel and bell pepper and cook, stirring occasionally, 2 minutes. Add the sausage and cook, stirring often, until it is browned, about 5 minutes. Carefully drain off any excess fat.

2 Add the eggplant, tomatoes, chicken stock, salt, and bay leaves to the pot. Bring to a boil. Reduce the heat to low, cover, and simmer gently for 30 minutes. Add the pasta and continue to cook, covered, until the pasta is tender, 25 to 30 minutes longer. Stir in the tomato, vinegar, and basil and remove from the heat. Remove and discard the bay leaves. Pass Parmesan cheese on the side.

2 tablespoons olive oil

1 large onion, diced

2 large garlic cloves, minced

1 small fresh chili pepper, preferably red, minced

1 small fennel bulb or 2 celery ribs, cut into ½-inch dice

1 large red bell pepper, diced

¾ pound Italian sausage, removed from the casing and crumbled

1 large eggplant (about 1 pound), peeled and cut into ½-inch dice

2 (14½-ounce) cans crushed tomatoes

3 cups chicken stock or reduced-sodium canned broth

½ teaspoon salt

2 bay leaves

1½ cups tiny pasta shells or ditalle

1 large tomato, coarsely chopped

1 tablespoon red wine vinegar

½ cup chopped fresh basil

Grated Parmesan cheese

Cuban Salmagundi

The annals of American cooking include an everything-but-the-kitchen-sink casserole called salmagundi. This casual Cuban dish is similar in that it, too, has a varied and sundry ingredient list. Diced avocado is a wonderfully indulgent garnish, but for the easiest of dinners, bring the dish to the table plain.

MAKES:
6 servings

PREP:
20 minutes

COOK:
1 hour

- 1 tablespoon olive oil
- 1 medium green bell pepper, chopped
- 1 medium onion, chopped

- 1½ pounds ground round beef
- ¾ pound bulk hot pork sausage
- 3 carrots, peeled and finely diced

- 2 large garlic cloves, minced
- 2 celery ribs, minced

- 1 (16-ounce) can black beans, rinsed and drained
- 1 (14½-ounce) can diced tomatoes, drained
- 1 (8-ounce) can tomato sauce
- 1 cup corn kernels
- 1 cup shredded Cheddar cheese, preferably white
- ¼ cup raisins
- ¼ cup pitted chopped green olives
- 1 teaspoon hot red pepper sauce, or to taste
- ½ teaspoon salt

- ½ cup crumbled queso fresco or shredded Monterey Jack cheese

1. Preheat the oven to 350° F. In a large flameproof casserole, heat the oil over high heat. Add the bell pepper and onion and cook, stirring often, until the vegetables are browned at the edges, 5 to 6 minutes. Remove the vegetables from the casserole, and set aside.

2. Add the ground beef, sausage, and carrots to the casserole. Reduce the heat to medium and cook, stirring to break up the meats, until they are no longer pink, 10 to 12 minutes. Drain off excess fat. Add the garlic and celery and cook 2 minutes. Return the vegetables to the casserole along with all the remaining ingredients except the queso fresco, and mix well.

3. Transfer the casserole to the oven and bake, uncovered, 40 minutes. Sprinkle the queso fresco over the top and return to the oven until the cheese is melted, about 5 minutes.

The flavor and texture of fresh corn is always superior to frozen or canned. Here's a simple way to **remove corn kernels**.

1. Husk the ear of corn and remove its silk.
2. Use a sharp knife to level the bottom of the stalk.
3. Stand the stalk on its cut end on top of a cutting board.
4. Use a paring or small serrated knife to cut down from the top of the stalk, keeping the blade close to the cob and letting the kernels fall on the cutting board.

Queso fresco, which means "fresh cheese" in Spanish, is a slightly salty, soft, fresh cheese made from cow's milk. Also known as queso blanco, this crumbly cheese is used to garnish many Mexican dishes, and can be found in tubs at Latin markets and in many large grocery stores.

Spring Lamb Navarin

Elegant and refined, this stew begins with lamb shanks, one of the richest and most full-flavored cuts. They're simmered to fall-off-the-bone tenderness, then mixed with a colorful mélange of baby spring vegetables for a light, delicate finish. The meat can be cooked a day or two ahead, making the final assembly pretty quick.

MAKES:
4 servings

PREP:
20 minutes

COOK:
2 hours,
30 minutes

2 tablespoons olive oil

3 large lamb shanks, excess fat trimmed

2 medium onions, sliced

4 garlic cloves, peeled and left whole

1 teaspoon dried thyme leaves

1 teaspoon dried rosemary

1¼ cups dry white wine

8 small white boiling onions or shallots, peeled

4 ounces baby carrots

4 ounces asparagus, trimmed and cut into 1½-inch lengths

4 ounces sugar snap peas

2 tablespoons flour

1 tablespoon unsalted butter

½ teaspoon salt

¼ teaspoon freshly ground pepper

¼ cup minced fresh mint, parsley, or chervil, or a combination

1 small tomato, seeded and finely diced

1 In a large sauté pan or Dutch oven, heat the olive oil over low heat. Add the lamb shanks, cover, and cook gently, turning occasionally, until no longer pink on the outside, taking care not to brown them too much, about 15 minutes.

2 Add the sliced onions, garlic, thyme, rosemary, and ½ cup of the wine, cover, and cook gently 30 minutes. Add the remaining ¾ cup wine and ¾ cup water and cook 1½ hours longer, turning the shanks several times. (The meat should be falling off the bones.) Remove from the heat.

3 Transfer the shanks to a cutting board. Strain the pan juices into a bowl and skim off the fat. When the shanks are cool enough to handle, remove the meat and cut into bite-size pieces. Set aside.

4 Meanwhile, partially fill the sauté pan with salted water and bring to a boil. Add the boiling onions and carrots and cook until the vegetables are partially tender, 5 to 7 minutes. Add the asparagus and sugar snap peas and cook until they are crisp-tender, 2 to 3 minutes. Drain.

5 In a small bowl, blend the flour with 2 tablespoons cold water to form a paste. Return the skimmed pan juices to the sauté pan. Slowly whisk in the flour mixture, bring to a boil, and cook 1 minute. Whisk in the butter, salt, and pepper. Return the meat and vegetables to the pan, add the mint and tomato, and cook until heated through, 3 to 5 minutes.

Navarin is derived from the French word *navet*, which means turnip. Traditionally, this was the stew's principal ingredient.

Boiling onions are small, white pungent onions slightly larger than pearl onions, about 1 inch in diameter. Cooks add them whole to soups, stews, and other dishes. With a rather hot flavor before cooking, these onions taste best whole. They also sometimes get pickled.

A mild herb related to parsley, **chervil** has a slight anise flavor. It is used extensively in French cuisine, and it is part of the popular spice mixture, *fines herbes*.

Persian Rice Cake with Lamb & Spinach

Middle Eastern cuisines have myriad ways of presenting rice that take it well beyond side-dish status. When cooked rice is formed into a cake and fried, it is called chelo. *When meat and vegetables are added, as they are here, it is known as* polo. *Either way, the cooking technique results in a wonderful contrast between the crisp bottom crust and the nicely steamed, soft top. Typically, a lot of butter has been added to reach this end, but a nonstick pan helps cut way back. Don't worry if some of the rice sticks to the pan—just pat it back into shape.*

MAKES:
6 servings

PREP:
10 minutes

COOK:
50 minutes

1½ **tablespoons olive oil**

1 **large onion, finely diced**

1 **pound lean ground lamb**

3 **large garlic cloves, minced**

1 **teaspoon ground cardamom**

1 **teaspoon ground paprika**

¼ **teaspoon cayenne**

¾ **teaspoon salt**

12 **ounces fresh spinach, washed, well-dried, and chopped**

2 **tablespoons minced fresh mint leaves**

3 **tablespoons unsalted butter**

6 **cups cooked basmati rice**

1 In a 10-inch nonstick sauté pan that is at least 3 inches deep or a nonstick Dutch oven, heat the olive oil over medium heat. Add the onion and cook, stirring often, until it begins to soften, 5 minutes. Add the lamb, garlic, cardamom, paprika, cayenne, and salt. Cook, stirring often, until the lamb is no longer pink, 6 to 8 minutes. Drain off any excess fat. Add the spinach to the pan and cook until it wilts, 2 to 3 minutes. Stir in the mint. Remove the mixture from the pan, and set aside. Wipe out the pan.

2 Melt the butter in the same pan, brushing it to coat the sides of the pan. Add half of the rice, forming an even layer that covers the entire bottom surface of the pan. Spoon the lamb mixture over the rice, spreading it evenly. Add the remaining rice, carefully spreading it over the lamb. Use the handle of a wooden spoon to make a hole through the center of the rice layer, going through to the bottom of the pan.

3 Cover the pan tightly and cook over medium-low heat for 35 minutes. Loosen the rice cake from the sides of the pan. Place a large serving platter over the pan and carefully invert the rice cake onto the platter. Serve hot or at room temperature.

Cardamom has a pungent aroma and a warm, spicy-sweet flavor with a eucalyptus-like kick. A member of the ginger family, this aromatic native of India also grows in many other tropical areas of the world. Cardamom seeds grow encapsulated in pods about the size of a cranberry, each containing about 20 tiny seeds. Cardamom must be hand-harvested, so it's relatively expensive.

You can purchase cardamom either in the pod or ground. Although more convenient, the latter form is not as full-flavored because cardamom seeds begin to lose their essential oils immediately upon grinding. If you buy a pod, you may remove the seeds, or grind the entire thing with a mortar and pestle. When using cardamom to flavor dishes, lightly crush the shell of the pod and add it and the seeds; the shell will disintegrate while the dish cooks. Practice frugality when using cardamom— a little goes a long way!

Orzo means barley in Italian, but it's actually a tiny, rice-shaped pasta. Orzo works perfectly in soups and is a wonderful substitute for rice.

Moroccan Veal Tagine with Orange & Cumin

Heady with a mix of spices and bountifully filled with vegetables, this North African stew is exotic enough to jazz up meals but still has a comfortingly familiar tenor.

MAKES:
4 to 6 servings

PREP:
15 minutes

COOK:
1 hour,
35 minutes

2   teaspoons ground cumin

1   teaspoon ground coriander

¾   teaspoon salt

¼   teaspoon cinnamon

¼   teaspoon cayenne

1½   pounds lean veal stew meat, cut into 1-inch cubes

2   tablespoons olive oil

1   large onion, diced

3   large carrots, peeled and sliced

8   large shallots, peeled

6   ounces small fresh mushrooms

2   large garlic cloves, minced

2   tablespoons red wine vinegar or sherry wine vinegar

1   cup chicken stock or reduced-sodium canned broth

½   cup orange juice

¼   cup tomato paste

1   tablespoon brown sugar

1   teaspoon minced lemon zest
    Freshly ground pepper

1 Preheat the oven to 350° F. In a small bowl, combine the cumin, coriander, salt, cinnamon, and cayenne; mix well. Sprinkle over the veal in a medium bowl and toss lightly to coat.

2 In a large nonreactive flameproof casserole, heat 1 tablespoon of the olive oil over high heat. Add the meat in batches and cook, turning occasionally, until browned on all sides, 6 to 8 minutes per batch. Remove the meat from the pan and set aside.

3 Heat the remaining 1 tablespoon olive oil in the casserole over medium-high heat. Add the onion, carrots, shallots, mushrooms, and garlic and cook, stirring often, until the onion begins to soften, 4 to 5 minutes.

4 Add the vinegar and stir up any browned bits from the bottom of the pan. Add the chicken stock, orange juice, tomato paste, and brown sugar and bring to a boil. Remove the casserole from the heat and add the meat.

5 Cover the casserole and transfer to the oven. Bake until the meat is tender, 1¼ to 1½ hours. Stir in the lemon zest and a generous amount of pepper just before serving.

Prized for cooking, the **shallot** has an especially rich, complex, subtle flavor that separates it from other types of onions. With papery brown skin and white flesh tinged with a rosy purple, its delicate flavor resembles a cross between sweet onion and garlic. Like the latter, the shallot's head is composed of multiple cloves, but they aren't covered in a sheath, making them easier to separate.

You'll find fresh green shallots in the spring, but, as with garlic and onions, dry shallots (with dry skins and moist flesh) are available all year. Choose plump, firm dry-skinned shallots with no signs of wrinkling or sprouting.

To peel and chop or mince shallots, peel the skin with a paring knife. Trim off a thin slice, and then set the shallot, cut side down, on a work surface. Make horizontal cuts toward the root, leaving it intact. Cut crosswise into pieces of desired fineness.

Lamb Stew with Orzo

Greek stifados, or stews, are similar to those that have graced the dinner table for generations. A subtle suggestion of sweet spices and often, the addition of tangy cheese, sets them apart.

MAKES:
4 to 6 servings

PREP:
10 minutes

COOK:
1 hour, 20 minutes

2	**tablespoons olive oil**
1	**cup orzo**
1¼	**teaspoons dried oregano**
1½	**pounds boneless leg of lamb, trimmed and cut into 1-inch cubes**
1	**medium onion, halved crosswise and each half cut into ½-inch wedges**
1	**large garlic clove, minced**
4	**whole cloves**
¼	**teaspoon cinnamon**
½	**teaspoon salt**
¼	**teaspoon freshly ground pepper**
1	**(14½-ounce) can diced tomatoes, juices reserved**
1	**tablespoon tomato paste**
1	**cup crumbled feta cheese**
2	**tablespoons minced fresh mint (optional)**

1 Preheat the oven to 350° F. In a large flameproof casserole, heat 1 tablespoon of the olive oil over high heat. Add the orzo and ¼ teaspoon of the oregano. Cook, stirring often, until the orzo is lightly toasted, 4 to 5 minutes. Remove the orzo from the pan and set it aside.

2 Heat the remaining 1 tablespoon olive oil in the same pan. Add the meat, in batches if necessary, and cook, turning occasionally, until browned on all sides, 6 to 8 minutes per batch.

3 Stir in the onion, garlic, cloves, cinnamon, salt, and pepper. Cook, stirring constantly, 1 minute longer. Add the tomatoes with their juices, 1 cup water, the tomato paste, and the reserved orzo. Mix well, cover tightly, and remove from the heat.

4 Transfer the casserole to the oven and bake 1 hour, or until the meat and pasta are tender, stirring once or twice and adding a little more water if the mixture seems too dry. Serve sprinkled with the cheese and mint.

Chili-Rubbed Lamb Shanks with Pinto Beans

Provençal French cooking long has celebrated the special affinity of lamb shanks and dried beans. The two seemingly disparate ingredients share their strengths with each other in a most agreeable way that isn't necessarily limited to French cooking. Southwestern ingredients are every bit as flattering.

MAKES:
4 servings

PREP:
10 minutes

COOK:
1 hour, 40 minutes

1 In a small bowl, combine 1 teaspoon of the adobo sauce, the orange juice, brown sugar, and cumin, and brush over the lamb shanks. In a large sauté pan or saucepan, heat the oil over medium-high heat. Add the shanks and cook, turning, until browned all over, 6 to 8 minutes. Add the onion and garlic and cook, stirring occasionally, until the onion begins to brown at the edges, about 3 minutes.

2 Add the chicken stock, tomatoes with their juices, and the remaining 2 teaspoons adobo sauce. Cover and bring to a boil. Reduce the heat to medium-low and simmer until the meat is tender, about 45 minutes.

3 Add the beans and continue to cook, covered, 45 minutes longer. Skim the fat from the surface. Stir in the minced chipotle pepper and salt, and serve.

1 canned chipotle chili pepper in adobo sauce, minced, plus 1 tablespoon adobo sauce from can

1 tablespoon orange juice

2 teaspoons brown sugar

1 teaspoon ground cumin

4 small lamb shanks (12 to 14 ounces each)

1½ tablespoons vegetable oil

1 medium onion, diced

2 large garlic cloves, minced

1¼ cups chicken stock or reduced-sodium canned broth

1 (14½-ounce) can diced tomatoes, juices reserved

1 (15-ounce) can pinto beans, rinsed and drained

¼ teaspoon salt

Osso Bucco

Classically Italian, this hearty and fragrant stew is enlivened with a few unconventional additions, such as sun-dried tomatoes and fresh basil. In Milan, it is often served with saffron-flavored risotto. Other options are cheese tortellini or a big, soft mound of polenta.

MAKES:
3 to 4 servings

PREP:
20 minutes

COOK:
2 hours,
10 minutes

3   tablespoons olive oil

4   large garlic cloves, halved

3   bay leaves

   Pinch of crushed hot red pepper

1   large onion, diced

2   small carrots, peeled and diced

2   small celery ribs, diced

4   veal shanks (3 to 4 pounds total), patted dry

½   teaspoon salt

¼   teaspoon freshly ground pepper

½   cup dry white wine

1½   teaspoons dried rosemary

1½   teaspoons dried basil

1   (28-ounce) can plum tomatoes, well-drained and diced

8   sun-dried tomatoes, chopped

1   cup beef stock or reduced-sodium canned broth

½   cup parsley sprigs

½   cup chopped fresh basil

1   teaspoon grated lemon zest

1 Preheat the oven to 350° F. In a large flameproof casserole, combine the olive oil, three-fourths of the garlic, the bay leaves, and hot red pepper. Cook over low heat, stirring often, until the garlic just begins to take on color, 1½ to 2 minutes. With a slotted spoon, remove the garlic and discard.

2 Increase the heat to medium-high. Add the onion, carrots, and celery to the casserole and cook, stirring often, until the vegetables begin to soften, 4 to 5 minutes. With a slotted spoon, remove the vegetables, letting the excess oil drip back into the pan. Add the veal shanks and season with the salt and pepper. Cook, turning, until browned on both sides, about 12 minutes. Set aside with the vegetables.

3 Add the wine, rosemary, and dried basil to the casserole and stir up the browned bits from the bottom of the pan. Bring to a boil and cook until the wine has almost fully evaporated, 4 to 5 minutes. Add the plum tomatoes and six of the sun-dried tomatoes and cook 2 minutes. Add the beef stock, shanks, and vegetables, and heat to a simmer.

4 Cover the casserole and transfer to the oven. Bake until the meat is tender, 1¾ to 2 hours. Remove and discard the bay leaves. Meanwhile, mince together the remaining garlic and sun-dried tomatoes with the parsley, fresh basil, and lemon zest. Sprinkle over the stew just before serving.

Made from sweet, dark red fruit, **sun-dried tomatoes** are sliced crosswise or halved, then dried in the sun to develop an intense sweet and tart flavor. They're found either packed in oil or dry in cellophane. Soak the dry type in liquid before use. To chop sun-dried tomatoes, slice them with a chef's knife, then gather the slices and cut across into pieces, or snip them with kitchen scissors.

Seafood offers a lighter touch to so many meals, and boasts of vibrancy, freshness, and versatility matched by few other foods. Of no small consequence are the healthy aspects of fish. With fewer calories and less fat than meat, fish has found a comfortable spot in most diets. And almost all fish and shellfish recipes cook fairly quickly, a bonus that's always appreciated.

There are so many ways to prepare fish. A rustic quality defines seafood stews, rich amalgams of fish set afloat in briny, sea-sweet broth. Almost every country that abuts an ocean or sea has a uniquely characteristic stew. **Italian Fish Stew with Vinegar-Glazed Leeks & Onions** is robust. **São Paulo Seafood Stew**, from Brazil, is more aggressively seasoned with delightful, aromatic notes that are ever so flattering to the seafood. A delicate hand dictates the character of many baked fish preparations, especially the **Niçoise-Style Haddock with Couscous** and the **Swordfish with Artichokes, Olives & Potatoes**. Bold Creole seasonings and touches of Tex-Mex also go admirably well with fish.

Seafood Dinners

Although air transport makes fresh fish much more available than ever, there will still be times when seasonal shortages may make it necessary to substitute other varieties of fish than those called for. This is when it pays to know your fishmonger, who likely can guide you to the most appropriate alternative choices. Frozen fish often is a fine option that can fill gaps in availability. When you buy frozen fish, take the time to rewrap it at home, or at the very least, add another layer of wrapping to protect it. Ice crystals will form in food that isn't wrapped properly, causing the quality to deteriorate quite noticeably. Thaw fish in the refrigerator, then carefully rinse it under cold water and pat dry before using.

Swordfish with Artichokes, Olives & Potatoes

Mediterranean influences abound here, from the briny sea-fresh taste of the swordfish to the piquancy of the capers and olives to the sunny touch that the artichokes add.

MAKES:
2 servings

PREP:
15 minutes

COOK:
25 minutes

1 Preheat the oven to 350° F. In a large ovenproof sauté pan or skillet, heat the olive oil over medium-high heat. Add the onion and garlic, and cook 1 minute. Add the potatoes, salt, and pepper. Cook, stirring often, until the potatoes begin to soften, 4 to 5 minutes. Add the wine, artichoke hearts, olives, and capers, and bring to a boil.

2 Place the fish in the pan, spooning the vegetable mixture aside so the fish is directly on the bottom of the pan. Cover tightly and transfer to the oven. Bake 17 to 20 minutes, or until the fish is cooked through. Sprinkle with the tomatoes, parsley, and a generous grinding of pepper, and serve at once.

2 tablespoons olive oil

1 small onion, chopped

1 large garlic clove, minced

4 tiny red potatoes, sliced

¼ teaspoon salt

¼ teaspoon freshly ground pepper

½ cup dry white wine

1 (6-ounce) jar marinated artichoke hearts, drained and patted dry

¼ cup French or other imported green olives

1 tablespoon capers

2 swordfish steaks (5 to 6 ounces each)

1 small plum tomato, seeded and finely diced

2 tablespoons minced parsley

Creole Court Bouillon

In the unique culinary vernacular of Creole cooking, this zesty dish of baked fish in tomato sauce has the same name as a delicate French fish poaching liquid. Name aside, there's no similarity. Like so many classic Creole dishes, this one is built upon a roux, onions, bell peppers, and celery.

MAKES:
4 servings

PREP:
15 minutes

COOK:
25 minutes

¼   **cup vegetable oil**

¼   **cup flour**

2   **large celery ribs, diced**

1   **large onion, diced**

1   **large green bell pepper, diced**

½   **cup red wine**

2½   **cups fish stock or broth**

1   **(14½-ounce) can diced tomatoes, drained**

2   **tablespoons Creole seasoning blend**

2   **bay leaves**

½   **teaspoon salt**

⅛   **teaspoon cayenne**

⅛   **teaspoon freshly ground black pepper**

4   **redfish, monkfish, or catfish fillets (4 to 5 ounces each)**

2   **scallions, sliced**

2   **tablespoons minced parsley**

1 In a large, deep sauté pan or large saucepan, heat the oil over medium-high heat. Gradually whisk in the flour and cook, stirring constantly, until it is a rich caramel color, 4 to 5 minutes. Immediately and carefully add the celery, onion, and bell pepper and cook, stirring often, 4 to 5 minutes.

2 Add the red wine and cook 30 seconds. Add the fish stock, tomatoes, Creole seasoning, bay leaves, and salt. Season with the cayenne and black pepper. Bring to a boil, reduce the heat to medium-low, and simmer, uncovered, 10 minutes.

3 Season the fish with salt, cayenne, and black pepper. Add the fish fillets to the pan, spooning some of the sauce over them. Cook gently until the fish flakes easily, 5 to 7 minutes. Stir in the scallions and remove from the heat.

4 To serve, transfer the fish to serving plates. Remove and discard the bay leaves and spoon the sauce over the fish. Garnish with the parsley.

Fish & Vegetables with Cilantro

Light and elegant, somewhere between a soup and a stew, this colorful and aromatic offering takes its character from a subtle layering of flavors. The cilantro, with its lacy leaves left whole, adds a fresh herbaceous aroma, the hot chili just a mild suggestion of its presence, and the fish its briny sustenance. In summer, when herb gardens have so much to offer, it will be tempting to add a few other fresh herbs, such as mint, basil, or even lemongrass, in addition to the cilantro.

MAKES:
3 to 4 servings
PREP:
20 minutes
COOK:
20 minutes

1 In a large saucepan, combine the fish stock, 1½ cups water, the wine, onion, shallots, garlic, and hot pepper. Bring to a boil, reduce the heat to medium-low, and simmer gently, uncovered, until the onion is softened, about 15 minutes.

2 Place the butter and cilantro in a tureen and set aside.

3 Add the zucchini and tomatoes to the broth and return it to a simmer. Add the fish, stirring gently so the pieces remain intact, and cook just until the fish turns opaque, 1 to 2 minutes. Stir in the vinegar and season with salt to taste. Pour the soup into the tureen, stir gently, and serve at once.

4   cups fish stock or clam juice

⅓   cup dry white wine

1   small onion, cut into ½-inch wedges

2   shallots, thinly sliced

2   medium garlic cloves, minced

1   small jalapeño or serrano pepper, seeded and thinly sliced

3   tablespoons unsalted butter, softened

1   cup cilantro leaves

2   small, slender zucchini, sliced

2   plum tomatoes, seeded and finely diced

1   pound firm, white-fleshed fish fillets, cut into 1¼-inch cubes

2   tablespoons seasoned rice vinegar
    Salt

Italian Fish Stew with Vinegar-Glazed Leeks & Onions

Any region of a country rimmed by water has at least one classic fish stew preparation. This is one of the lesser-known types from Italy, a superb rendition that has a substantive base of slow-cooked, vinegar-glazed onions. It can be made ahead of time, up to the point of adding the fish, offering a practical solution to last-minute meals.

MAKES:
4 servings

PREP:
25 minutes

COOK:
40 minutes

⅔ cup high-quality red wine vinegar
1 tablespoon balsamic vinegar

1 small branch of fresh rosemary or
   1 teaspoon dried
2 small leeks, trimmed and sliced
1 medium onion, cut into thin wedges
1 garlic clove, sliced paper thin

¼ cup olive oil
½ teaspoon salt
⅛ teaspoon freshly ground pepper

1 (14½-ounce) can diced tomatoes, juices
   reserved, or 2 cups diced fresh tomatoes

1 cup dry white wine
2½ cups fish stock or clam juice

½ pound shelled and deveined shrimp
½ pound scallops
½ pound firm, white-fleshed fish,
   cut into 1¼-inch chunks

2 tablespoons minced parsley
1 teaspoon minced lemon zest

1 In a large, nonreactive flameproof casserole or saucepan, combine the red wine and balsamic vinegars, and bring to a boil. Add the rosemary, leeks, onion, and garlic. Cover, reduce the heat to low, and simmer, stirring occasionally, 15 minutes. Uncover, increase the heat to high, and cook, stirring often, until the vinegar is almost completely cooked away, 5 to 6 minutes.

2 With the heat still on high, and the olive oil, ¼ teaspoon of the salt, and the pepper. Cook, stirring often, 2 minutes. Reduce the heat to low, and cook, stirring often, until the onions are very soft, 3 to 4 minutes. Add the tomatoes with their juices and simmer 2 to 3 minutes. Add the wine, fish stock, and remaining ¼ teaspoon salt and heat to a simmer. Cook 5 minutes. Remove and discard the fresh rosemary.

3 Add the shrimp, scallops, and fish. Cook gently until the fish is just opaque throughout, about 5 minutes. Add the parsley and lemon zest and season with additional pepper to taste. Serve at once.

Niçoise-Style Haddock with Couscous

Couscous is an invaluable addition to the pantry. Best known as a Moroccan ingredient, it is endlessly adaptable to many cuisines. But perhaps its most notable traits are how quickly it can be prepared and how easily it can be added to baked dishes and stews. Here, it is flavored with some of the same ingredients that sauces pan-cooked fish fillets.

MAKES:
2 to 3 servings

PREP:
15 minutes

COOK:
20 minutes

1 In a large sauté pan or skillet, heat the olive oil over medium-high heat. Add the leek, fennel, and garlic and cook, stirring often, until the leek is tender, 4 to 5 minutes. Add the tomatoes with their juices, the wine, bay leaf, orange zest, thyme, salt, and cayenne, and bring to a boil.

2 Place the couscous in a medium bowl. Spoon about ¾ cup of the tomato mixture into the couscous, making sure to get some of the loose liquid in addition to the chunky vegetables. Add 2 tablespoons hot water, cover tightly, and let stand while you cook the fish.

3 Add the fish to the tomato mixture left in the pan, spooning the sauce over the fish. Cover and simmer until the fish is cooked through, 8 to 10 minutes. Remove and discard the bay leaf. Add the olives. Fluff the couscous with a fork. Spoon onto plates and top with the fish and sauce.

1   tablespoon olive oil

1   medium leek (white and tender green), cleaned, trimmed, and chopped

½   of a medium fennel bulb, chopped

1   large garlic clove, minced

1   (14½-ounce) can diced tomatoes, juices reserved

¼   cup dry white wine

1   bay leaf

1   teaspoon finely grated orange zest

½   teaspoon dried thyme leaves

½   teaspoon salt

¼   teaspoon cayenne

½   cup couscous

12   ounces haddock, cod, or scrod, cut into 2 or 3 fillets

¼   cup Niçoise or other imported black olives

Red Snapper Creole

During a visit to Chicago, noted chef Paul Prudhomme explained that the proper Creole sauce should be the color of burnished copper or like "gorgeous red hair."
This rendition, with a smoky backdrop of bacon and moderate level of spice,
is right on target all around, from the color to the spicy flavor.

MAKES
6 to 8 servings
PREP:
20 minutes
COOK:
25 minutes

3	bacon slices, preferably applewood-smoked
1/8	teaspoon cayenne
1½	tablespoons vegetable oil
1	medium onion, cut into ½-inch dice
1	large green bell pepper, cut into ½-inch dice
2	celery ribs, diced
3½	tablespoons flour
1	(15-ounce) can tomato sauce
2 to 3	teaspoons Creole seasoning blend
½	teaspoon dried thyme leaves
½	teaspoon sugar
4	ounces andouille sausage or other spicy smoked sausage, sliced

1	pound red snapper, cut into 1-inch strips, or 1 pound large peeled and deveined shrimp
1	large tomato, cut into ¼-inch dice
	Hot red pepper sauce
3 to 4	cups cooked white rice

1 Rub the bacon with the cayenne; dice the bacon. In a large, heavy saucepan, heat the oil over medium-high heat. Add the bacon and cook, stirring often, until browned, about 4 minutes. Add the onion, bell pepper, and celery and cook, stirring, until the vegetables begin to soften, 2 to 3 minutes. Reduce the heat to medium and continue to cook until the vegetables are soft, about 4 minutes. Sprinkle on the flour and stir in. Cook, stirring constantly, 1 minute. Stir in 1¼ cups hot water.

2 Add the tomato sauce, Creole seasoning, thyme, sugar, and sausage. Cover and cook over low heat 10 minutes. Add the fish and tomato and cook just until the fish turns opaque, about 3 minutes. Season with hot sauce to taste and serve over the rice.

Grecian Isles Baked Shrimp with Feta & Tomatoes

With its symphony of flavors and textures, this dish approaches the status of a classic. Every ingredient makes its own statement, from the buttery bread crumbs to the salty tang of the cheese and the quiet hint of heat from the hot red pepper. If you have six individual gratin dishes, divide the mixture among them before baking for an elegant presentation.

MAKES:
6 servings
PREP:
10 minutes
COOK:
30 minutes

1 Preheat the oven to 375° F. In a large ovenproof skillet or flameproof gratin pan, melt 2 tablespoons of the butter over high heat. Add the bread crumbs and cook, stirring often, until they begin to crisp, 3 to 4 minutes. Remove from the pan and set aside.

2 Add the remaining 1 tablespoon butter to the same pan along with the olive oil, salt, and hot red pepper. Cook over high heat until the butter sizzles. Add the shrimp and garlic in batches if necessary and cook, stirring occasionally, just until the shrimp turn pink, 4 to 5 minutes per batch.

3 Stir in the wine and boil until it thickens slightly, 3 to 4 minutes. Remove from the heat and stir in the tomatoes. Sprinkle with the feta cheese and dill, then top with the bread crumbs. Transfer the pan to the oven and bake 12 to 15 minutes, or just until bubbly.

3 **tablespoons unsalted butter**
¼ **cup fresh bread crumbs**

2 **tablespoons olive oil**
½ **teaspoon salt**
⅛ **teaspoon crushed hot red pepper**

2 **pounds peeled jumbo or large shrimp, tails left attached**
2 **large garlic cloves, minced**

⅔ **cup dry white wine**

2 **medium tomatoes, seeded and diced**

3 **ounces crumbled feta cheese, plain or with cracked pepper**
2 **tablespoons minced fresh dill**

Sicilian Tuna with Fettuccine & Melting Onions

There's a quiet but wonderfully orchestrated harmony of flavors at work in this dish, with the sweet-and-sour onions playing off the richness of the tuna, the pungent freshness of the mint, and the saltiness of the capers. Unlike so many pasta dishes, this one can be served hot or at room temperature, easing the burden of last-minute work.

MAKES:
4 servings

PREP:
10 minutes

COOK:
30 minutes

2 medium onions, cut into thin wedges

½ cup dry white wine

5 tablespoons olive oil, preferably extra virgin

3 to 4 tablespoons wine vinegar

1 tablespoon honey

¼ teaspoon salt

⅛ teaspoon freshly ground pepper

3 tablespoons flour

4 fresh tuna steaks (about 6 ounces each), cut ¾ inch thick

¼ cup fresh mint leaves, cut into thin strips, plus several sprigs for garnish

12 ounces dried fettuccine, freshly cooked
Grated zest and juice of ½ lemon
Pinch of crushed hot red pepper

1 tablespoon drained capers

1 In a large nonstick skillet, combine the onions, ½ cup water, the wine, and 2 tablespoons of the olive oil. Cook over high heat until most of the liquid has cooked away, 10 to 15 minutes. Reduce the heat to medium-low, and cook gently until the onions begin to caramelize, 7 to 10 minutes.

2 Add 3 tablespoons of the vinegar, the honey, salt, and pepper. Cook, stirring often, until the onions are nicely glazed, about 5 minutes, adding the remaining vinegar as necessary to reach the desired balance of sweet and sour. Transfer to a bowl and cover to keep warm.

3 Place the flour on a plate and season lightly with additional salt and pepper. Coat both sides of the tuna with the flour mixture. Heat 1 tablespoon of the olive oil in the skillet over high heat. Add the tuna and cook, turning once, until browned outside and cooked through, about 5 minutes for medium-rare or longer to desired doneness. Sprinkle the mint over the fish and spoon the hot onions over.

4 To serve, toss the hot pasta with the remaining 2 tablespoons olive oil, the lemon rind, lemon juice, and hot red pepper. Divide among four plates and top with a portion of the tuna and onions. Sprinkle with the capers and serve hot or at room temperature, garnished with the mint sprigs.

Using good **vinegar** is essential so the taste will be mellow and soft rather than astringent. Several types mixed together are ideal. Start with a nice red wine vinegar and add some sherry vinegar or white wine vinegar. If you use balsamic, keep it to about 2 teaspoons of the total, or it will be too dominant.

There are numerous varieties of **tuna**; the best-known include albacore, blue fin, yellow fin, and bonito. All tunas have a moderate to high fat content, with a distinctively rich-flavored flesh that's firmly textured, flaky, and tender. Found in temperate waters around the globe, tuna is a member of the mackerel family. Depending on the variety, fresh tuna is available seasonally from late spring to early fall. Frozen tuna is available anytime, sold in both steaks and fillets.

In Greek mythology, the nymph Mentha angered Pluto's wife Persephone, and got turned into an aromatic plant. **Mint** is a sweet, refreshing, and invigorating herb available in more than 30 varieties, with spearmint and peppermint the most popular. Of the two, peppermint is the more pungent, with bright green leaves, purple-tinged stems, and a peppery flavor. The gray-green or true green leaves of spearmint have a milder flavor and fragrance. Mint grows wild all over the planet, and it's exceptionally easy to grow. When buying it from a market, choose evenly colored leaves with no sign of wilting.

São Paulo Seafood Stew

Brazilian influences define this soup and set it apart from some of the more familiar seafood-based main-course soups. The pungent perfume of coriander, the fresh fillip of lime, and the seductive richness of coconut milk make it memorable.

MAKES:
4 servings

PREP:
10 minutes

COOK:
30 minutes

2 tablespoons unsalted butter

1 medium onion, cut into ½-inch dice

2 small bell peppers, preferably 1 red and 1 green, cut into ½-inch dice

1½ teaspoons ground coriander

2 large garlic cloves, minced

1 small jalapeño pepper, minced

3 cups fish stock

1 (14½-ounce) can diced tomatoes, drained

Juice of 1 large lime

½ teaspoon salt

½ cup canned unsweetened coconut milk

12 small clams, scrubbed

½ pound sea scallops

12 ounces sea bass or other firm, white-fleshed fish, cut into 1¼-inch chunks

¼ cup minced cilantro

1 In a large saucepan, melt the butter over medium heat. Add the onion, bell peppers, and coriander. Reduce the heat to medium-low and cook gently, stirring occasionally, until the vegetables are softened, 6 to 8 minutes. Add the garlic and jalapeño pepper and cook 1 minute longer. Add the fish stock, tomatoes, lime juice, and salt. Bring to a boil, cover, and simmer 10 minutes.

2 Stir in the coconut milk and return to a simmer. Add the clams, cover, and simmer until the shells begin to open, 4 to 5 minutes. Add the scallops and sea bass and simmer, uncovered, until all the seafood is opaque throughout, 3 to 5 minutes. Do not overcook. Stir in the cilantro just before serving.

Mussels with Chorizo, Corn & Tomatoes

Generously imbued with the briny sweetness of the sea, mussels are succulent and surprisingly inexpensive. Much of the supply now is farm-raised, bringing forth a bounty of small, mildly flavored, and clean mussels so they're even better than ever. Many recipes hone in on the French influences, but here Tex-Mex tastes add just the right touch.

MAKES:
2 to 3 servings
PREP:
20 minutes
COOK:
15 minutes

1 In a large nonreactive saucepan, combine the sausage, onion, bell pepper, and chili powder, and cook over medium-high heat, stirring often, until the onion and pepper are softened, 5 minutes. Stir in the vinegar and wine, then the mussels.

2 Cover and cook over high heat until all the mussels have opened, 4 to 5 minutes. Add the tomatoes and corn and season with pepper to taste. Reduce the heat to low and cook, uncovered, 1 minute. Sprinkle with cilantro and serve at once.

3 ounces Mexican chorizo or hot Italian sausage, removed from the casing and crumbled

1 medium onion, chopped

1 red bell pepper, cut into 1/4-inch dice

1/4 teaspoon chili powder

1 tablespoon white wine vinegar

2/3 cup dry white wine

2 pounds mussels, cleaned

2 medium tomatoes, coarsely chopped

1 cup corn kernels

Freshly ground pepper

Chopped cilantro (optional)

Pasta has developed a depth and diversity that few other foods can claim. Most stores carry a surprising array of shapes and sizes, while the best suppliers have everything from fresh to frozen, filled to dried. It's no longer enough to look just in the pasta aisle, since the freezer, refrigerator case, and often the deli area are also apt to have some tempting pasta choices.

Pasta Dinners

Pasta dresses up or down with equal ease and is always amenable to last-minute meals. For fancy, look to **Gnocchi with Wild Mushroom Broth, Pasta with Scallops & Salad Greens in Creamy Tarragon Dressing**, or **Seafood Pasta Primavera**. A more casual attitude comes across in **Baked Tortellini with Tomatoes & Cheese** and **Andrew's Ready Spaghetti**. When simplicity is called for, **Penne with Tomatoes, Mint & Sage** and **Pasta with Broccoli Rabe & Tomatoes** are easy, timesaving answers.

The last-minute cooking aspects of pasta can seem to be a deterrent to easy meals. But in many cases where the pasta is tossed into a sauce, it can be cooked ahead of time so the last-minute juggling act can be put to rest. There are also several recipes in this chapter that combine two steps into one, making pasta easier than ever. It is sometimes possible to cook pasta and sauce together in one easy step for a welcome savings in time and cleanup.

Pasta with Broccoli Rabe & Tomatoes

Broccoli rabe, also called "rapini," has an appealing bitter edge. In this dish, it is tamed by white beans and matched in vigor by lots of garlic and crushed hot red pepper.

MAKES:
4 servings
PREP:
15 minutes
COOK:
20 minutes

1. In a large saucepan, cook the pasta according to package directions until tender but still firm, about 10 minutes. Drain. Transfer the pasta to a large serving bowl or platter. Add ½ tablespoon of the olive oil and toss gently to coat.

2. Heat 1½ tablespoons of the olive oil in the saucepan over medium-high heat. Add the bread crumbs and cook, stirring constantly, until crisp and browned, 2 to 3 minutes. Remove the bread crumbs from the pan and set aside.

3. Heat the remaining olive oil in the saucepan over medium heat. Add the garlic, onion, hot red pepper, and ¼ teaspoon of the salt. Cook, stirring often, until the onion is softened, 3 to 5 minutes. Increase the heat to high. Add the broccoli rabe and cook, stirring often, until the broccoli rabe is wilted, about 2 minutes. Add the beans, tomatoes, chicken stock, and remaining ¼ teaspoon salt. Cook, stirring occasionally, until heated through, 3 to 4 minutes.

4. Spoon the sauce over the pasta. Sprinkle with the Parmesan cheese and the bread crumbs and serve.

8	ounces medium pasta shells or penne
¼	cup olive oil
¼	cup fresh bread crumbs
2	large garlic cloves, minced
1	small onion, chopped
½	teaspoon crushed hot red pepper
½	teaspoon salt
1	large bunch of broccoli rabe, coarsely chopped
1¼	cups white beans, such as Great Northern or cannellini (cooked dried beans or canned)
1½	cups chopped tomatoes
¼	cup chicken stock or reduced-sodium canned broth
¼	cup shaved or freshly grated Parmesan cheese

Pasta with Scallops & Salad Greens in Creamy Tarragon Dressing

*French influences abound in this delicate and light mix of pasta with greens.
Most markets now sell mixed salad greens that include
some bitter ones such as chicory and rocket. Whatever you select,
try to include some sharp-flavored greens for contrast.*

MAKES:
3 to 4 servings
PREP:
20 minutes
COOK:
25 minutes

5	tablespoons olive oil
1	tablespoon fresh lemon juice
1	tablespoon sherry vinegar
1	tablespoon minced fresh tarragon or 1½ teaspoons dried
½	teaspoon salt
¼	teaspoon pepper

8	ounces fettuccine

1	cup dry white wine
3	large shallots, minced
½	of a small red bell pepper, finely diced

½	cup heavy cream

2	cups mesclun or mixed salad greens
1	small Belgian endive, cut into matchstick pieces

12	ounces sea scallops, cut in half crosswise and patted dry

1	small tomato, seeded and finely diced

1 For the dressing, combine 3 tablespoons of the olive oil, the lemon juice, vinegar, 2 teaspoons of the fresh tarragon or 1 teaspoon of the dried, ¼ teaspoon of the salt, and ⅛ teaspoon of the black pepper in a small bowl.

2 In a large flameproof casserole, cook the fettuccine, according to package directions, until tender but still firm, about 10 minutes. Drain the fettuccine and transfer to a large bowl. Add 1 tablespoon of the olive oil and toss lightly to coat. Cover with foil to keep warm and set aside.

3 Add the wine, shallots, and bell pepper to the casserole. Cook, stirring occasionally, over high heat until most of the wine has cooked away, 4 to 5 minutes. Add 2 tablespoons of the dressing and the cream. Boil until slightly thickened, about 2 minutes.

4 Add the shallot cream to the hot pasta along with the salad greens and endive. Toss gently to mix. Cover and set aside.

5 Heat the remaining 1 tablespoon olive oil in the casserole over high heat. Add the scallops and the remaining 1/4 teaspoon salt and 1/8 teaspoon pepper. Cook just until the scallops are firm, about 2 minutes. Add the remaining dressing and toss gently to mix.

6 To serve, transfer the pasta mixture to a platter and arrange the scallops around the edge. Garnish with the tomato and remaining tarragon.

Scallops come in many species, but are generally classified into two broad groups—bay scallops and sea scallops. Bay scallops have sweeter, more succulent meat; they are quite small, with the muscle measuring about 1/2 inch in diameter. The muscle of the larger, more widely available sea scallop averages 1 1/2 inches in diameter and is not as tender as the smaller varieties. Though slightly chewier, the meat is still sweet and moist. Scallops range in color from pale beige to creamy pink. Stark white scallops have been soaked in water to increase their weight. Scallops perish quickly out of water, so they're usually sold shucked. All fresh scallops should have a sweet smell and a fresh, moist sheen.

The **endive** appeared quite by accident when a Belgian farmer threw chicory from his coffee on a dirt floor in his barn, and later discovered that blanched plants had emerged from the earth. Although he was immediately impressed by the flavor, it took 30 years before endive became a commercial crop. Smooth, slender, and compact, Belgian endives have bright white, yellow-tipped leaves with a rich, slightly bitter flavor. Once difficult to find in stores, today this versatile vegetable has become the darling of inspired chefs and creative cooks.

Orzo with Vegetable Tomato Sauce & Pesto

Vibrant with the colors and flavors of summer, this simple pasta dish couldn't be much easier to prepare. The little, rice-shaped pasta doesn't have to be cooked separately from the sauce. Instead, it simmers to the perfect consistency right along with all the other ingredients.

MAKES:
2 to 3 servings
PREP:
15 minutes
COOK:
30 minutes

2   **small bell peppers, one red and one yellow, or two red**

2   **tablespoons olive oil**
1   **medium red onion, chopped**
1   **large garlic clove, minced**

1   **small zucchini, finely diced**
¼   **pound fresh mushrooms, diced**

1   **cup orzo**
¼   **cup dry red wine**
1   **(14½-ounce) can diced tomatoes, juices reserved**
¼   **teaspoon salt**

3   **tablespoons pesto sauce, homemade or purchased**
   Freshly ground black pepper

   Grated Parmesan cheese

1 Arrange the peppers on a baking sheet and broil, turning, until blackened all over, about 10 minutes. Alternately, roast by charring directly over a gas flame. Transfer the roasted peppers to a paper bag, seal tightly, and let stand 10 minutes to loosen the skin. Slip off the blackened skin and remove the core and seeds. Cut the peppers into ½-inch dice.

2 In a large saucepan, preferably nonstick, heat the oil over medium-high heat. Add the onion and garlic and cook, stirring often, until the onion begins to soften, 3 to 4 minutes. Add the zucchini and mushrooms and cook 2 minutes longer. Stir in the orzo, wine, tomatoes with their juices, 1 cup water, and the salt.

3 Cover and bring to a boil. Reduce the heat to low and simmer gently, stirring often, until the pasta is almost tender, about 10 minutes. Remove from the heat.

4 Add the roasted peppers, cover, and let stand 5 minutes. Stir in the pesto sauce and pepper to taste. Serve with Parmesan cheese.

Gnocchi with Wild Mushroom Broth

Gnocchi, little Italian potato dumplings, are the perfect vehicle for this lusty, woodsy sauce. Many supermarkets that have fresh pasta carry them, but if they aren't available, use penne or ziti instead.

MAKES:
3 to 4 servings
PREP:
15 minutes
COOK:
20 minutes

1 In a large pot, cook the gnocchi according to package directions until tender but still firm, 4 to 5 minutes. Drain. Transfer the gnocchi to a medium bowl. Add the olive oil and toss lightly to coat. Cover with foil to keep warm and set aside.

2 Add the butter to the pot and melt over medium heat. Add the garlic, tomatoes, and half of the rosemary and cook, stirring often, until the garlic is softened, 3 to 5 minutes, watching carefully so it does not begin to color. Add the mushrooms, zucchini, nutmeg, salt, and pepper. Cook, stirring often, until the mushrooms begin to wilt, about 4 minutes.

3 Add the chicken and veal stocks and simmer until the mushrooms are tender, about 5 minutes. Stir in the remaining rosemary. To serve, divide the gnocchi among three to four shallow pasta bowls. Top with the mushroom mixture and sprinkle with the cheese.

1   **pound potato gnocchi**

1   **tablespoon olive oil**

7   **tablespoons unsalted butter**
4   **large garlic cloves, minced**
4   **sun-dried tomato halves, minced**
2   **tablespoons minced fresh rosemary or 1 teaspoon dried**

1   **pound mixed wild mushrooms (shiitakes, chanterelles, cremini, or porcini), halved or sliced**
1   **small zucchini, finely diced**
1/8   **teaspoon freshly grated nutmeg**
1/2   **teaspoon salt**
1/4   **teaspoon pepper**

1 1/2   **cups chicken stock or reduced-sodium canned broth**
1   **cup veal stock, beef stock, or canned broth**

1/3   **cup grated Parmesan cheese**

Vegetable Lasagna

Vegetables replace meat in this lush layering that includes three types of cheese, fresh basil pesto sauce, and a creamy béchamel sauce. There are lots of shortcuts that can be called on to streamline the preparation. A light tomato sauce, pesto sauce, and Alfredo sauce can all be selected from the refrigerator case at the market instead of making them from scratch, if desired. There are two methods given for cooking the eggplant. Sautéed, it has a richer taste, derived from the additional olive oil. Boiled, it cuts back on some of the fat.

MAKES:
6 to 8 servings

PREP:
15 minutes

SOAK & DRAIN:
30 minutes

COOK:
1 hour, 10 minutes

STAND:
10 minutes

1	large eggplant, cut into ½-inch round slices
	Salt
½	ounce dried imported mushrooms
4 to 6	tablespoons olive oil
2	large bell peppers, one yellow and one red, or two red
1	large onion, halved crosswise, then cut into thin wedges
4	precooked lasagna noodles
3	cups marinara or red sauce
½	cup grated Parmesan cheese
¼ to ½	teaspoon crushed hot red pepper, to taste

1	pound ricotta cheese
1	cup béchamel sauce or Alfredo sauce
⅓	cup pesto sauce
1½	cups shredded mozzarella cheese

1 Place the eggplant in a colander, sprinkle lightly with salt, and let drain 30 minutes. Blot the eggplant dry. Meanwhile, place the dried mushrooms in a small bowl and cover with boiling water. Let stand 20 minutes and drain.

2 Preheat the oven to 350° F. In a large skillet, heat 2 tablespoons of the olive oil over high heat. Add the bell peppers and onion and cook, stirring often, until the peppers begin to soften, 3 to 5 minutes. Cover, reduce the heat to medium-low, and cook, stirring occasionally, until the peppers are tender, about 10 minutes. Add the drained mushrooms and cook 2 minutes longer. Remove to a bowl.

3 To fry the eggplant, heat 2 tablespoons oil over high heat. Add the eggplant in batches and cook, turning once, until the eggplant is tender, 4 to 5 minutes, adding additional oil as necessary. Transfer the eggplant to paper towels. Or, to boil the eggplant, bring a large pan of water to a boil. Add the eggplant and cook until it is tender but not soggy, 5 minutes. Drain well and blot dry, removing as much water as possible.

4 Place one lasagna noodle in a 9-inch square baking pan. Spread with some of the marinara sauce and sprinkle lightly with half the Parmesan cheese and the hot red pepper. Add half of the eggplant, and then top with half of the bell pepper mixture. Dot with half of the ricotta. Add another lasagna noodle and some more marinara sauce. Add the remaining eggplant, then the remaining bell pepper mixture. Sprinkle with hot red pepper. Add the béchamel and top with small spoonfuls of pesto sauce. Add the remaining ricotta and some marinara sauce. Add the last lasagna noodle, spread with marinara sauce, and sprinkle with the mozzarella cheese and the remaining Parmesan cheese.

5 Cover with aluminum foil and bake 40 minutes. Remove the foil and continue to bake until the lasagna is hot in the center, 10 to 15 minutes. Let stand 10 minutes before cutting to serve.

Most **precooked lasagna noodles** are sold in sheets rather than the more familiar long noodles. Each sheet fits comfortably in a 9-inch square pan. If you have long noodles, use enough to make four layers, cutting them as necessary to fit the pan. If precooked lasagna noodles aren't available, cook dried lasagna noodles according to package directions before assembling.

The word **ricotta** means "re-cooked," and derives from the process in which the cheese is made by heating the whey from another cooked cheese. Ricotta serves as an ingredient in many Italian savory preparations such as lasagna and manicotti, as well as in desserts like cannoli and cheesecake. Ricotta is soft, smooth, light, and mild. Traditionally made from twice-cooked sheep's milk, cow's milk ricotta is now far more common. Whole milk or part-skim products are available, sold in small tubs in most grocery stores. For best quality, seek out fresh ricotta from Italian delicatessens.

Béchamel, the base of many other sauces, was named after its inventor, Louis de Béchamel, steward to Louis XIV. This basic French white sauce is made by stirring milk into a butter-flour roux. The thickness of the sauce depends on the proportion of flour and butter to milk; proportions for a thin sauce would be 1 tablespoon each of butter and flour to 1 cup of milk; a sauce of medium consistency would use 2 tablespoons each of butter and flour; a thick sauce, 3 tablespoons of each.

Ragout of Fresh Clams with Artichokes & Tomatoes

Whether they're steamed and eaten whole or pared down to the tender inner bottoms that are so rigorously protected by a thorny choke, artichokes require a certain amount of fortitude. But they're always worth the effort. Here, they're paired with fresh clams, tomatoes, and a good dose of garlic as a topping for pasta.

MAKES:
4 servings

PREP:
25 minutes

COOK:
20 minutes

4	medium to large artichokes
1	lemon
¼	cup olive oil
¾	cup fresh bread crumbs
1	small onion, finely diced
3	large garlic cloves, minced
3	medium tomatoes, peeled, seeded, and chopped
1	spring of fresh thyme or a pinch of dried
1	cup homemade fish stock, light chicken stock, or reduced-sodium canned chicken broth
¼	cup dry white wine or dry vermouth
¼ to ½	teaspoon crushed hot red pepper, to taste

2	dozen small clams, well scrubbed
2	tablespoons minced fresh basil
	Salt and freshly ground black pepper
1	pound hot cooked linguine or spaghetti

1 With a small sharp knife, cut away the top of each artichoke. Cut a flat bottom on each, and then peel away all the leaves from the bottoms. Remove the fuzzy choke and trim the bottoms down to a neat white portion. Cut the lemon in half and squeeze the juice of one half into a small bowl of water. Add the artichoke bottoms to the water as they are peeled to keep them from discoloring.

2 In a large skillet, heat 2 tablespoons of the olive oil over medium-high heat. Add the bread crumbs and cook, stirring constantly, until they are crisp, 2 to 3 minutes. Remove the bread crumbs from the skillet and set aside.

3 Heat the remaining 2 tablespoons olive oil in the same skillet. Add the onion and garlic and cook, stirring often, until they begin to soften, 3 to 5 minutes, watching closely so the garlic does not brown. Add the tomatoes, thyme, fish stock, wine, and hot red pepper. Remove the artichokes from the water, cut into six wedges each, and add them to the skillet. Cover and bring to a boil. Reduce the heat to medium-low and simmer until the artichokes are tender, 12 to 15 minutes.

4 Arrange the clams atop the vegetable mixture in the skillet. Cover and cook over medium-high heat just until all the clams have opened, 3 to 5 minutes. Add the basil and season with salt and pepper to taste.

5 To serve, divide the linguine among 4 shallow soup or pasta bowls and top with a portion of the clams and sauce. Cut the other half of the lemon into wedges and add one to each bowl. Sprinkle with the bread crumbs and serve at once.

Deriving from the French verb *ragoûter* meaning to stimulate the appetite, **ragout** is a thick, rich, well-seasoned stew of meat, poultry, or fish to which vegetables can be added.

Clams are grayish tan bivalve mollusks with sweet, tender flesh, available live in the shell or already shucked. Native Americans used parts of the shell to make wampum—beads used in barter, ornament, and for ceremonial or spiritual purposes.

You can cook clams in a variety of ways, including steaming and baking, but they should be cooked gently to prevent toughening. When buying hard-shell clams in the shell, make sure the shells are tightly closed and discard all cooked clams that did not open. Store live clams up to two days in the refrigerator; shucked clams will keep in the fridge for up to four days.

To scrub clams, soak them for several minutes generously covered in cold water. Then, under cold running water, scrub the shells clean with a small, stiff-bristled brush.

Pasta with Chicken, Greens & Herbed Cheese

Loaded with garlic-and-herb cheese and tossed with tender greens and bits of chicken, this pasta dish is unapologetically rich and indulgent splurge for special times.

MAKES:
2 to 3 servings

PREP:
15 minutes

COOK:
15 minutes

8	ounces rigatoni or penne
1½	teaspoons olive oil
1	tablespoon unsalted butter
1½	cups shredded cooked chicken
4	ounces garlic-and-herb flavored soft-spread cheese
1	cup chicken stock or reduced-sodium canned broth
6	sun-dried tomato halves, cut into slivers
½	teaspoon dried rosemary
⅔	cup coarsely chopped watercress
2	scallions, thinly sliced
¼	teaspoon salt
⅛	teaspoon pepper

Grated Parmesan cheese

1 In a large saucepan, cook the rigatoni, according to package directions, until tender but still firm, about 10 minutes. Drain. Transfer the rigatoni to a medium bowl. Add the olive oil and toss lightly to coat.

2 Melt the butter in the saucepan over high heat. Add the chicken and cook, stirring occasionally, until heated through, 1 to 2 minutes. Add the cheese, chicken stock, sun-dried tomatoes, and rosemary. Reduce the heat to low and cook, stirring, until the cheese is melted, about 1 minute.

3 Gently stir in the rigatoni, watercress, scallions, salt, and pepper. Cook just until heated through, 2 to 3 minutes. Serve sprinkled with the Parmesan cheese.

Penne with Tomatoes, Mint & Sage

This is another very simple offering when "quick" needs to be a key operative.

MAKES:
3 to 4 servings

PREP:
10 minutes

COOK:
20 minutes

1 | In a large saucepan, combine the tomato sauce and 3½ cups water and bring to a boil. Add the pasta and hot red pepper, cover, and cook over low heat until the pasta is tender, 15 to 18 minutes, stirring often, especially toward the end of cooking.

2 | When the pasta is cooked, remove the pan from the heat and add the tomato, sage, mint, olive oil, vinegar, and salt. Season with black pepper to taste. Pass a bowl of grated Romano cheese on the side.

1 **(15-ounce) can tomato sauce**

12 **ounces penne**
Pinch of crushed hot red pepper

1 **large tomato, seeded and diced**
2 **tablespoons minced fresh sage**
1 **tablespoon minced fresh mint**
2 **tablespoons olive oil**
2 **teaspoons balsamic or red wine vinegar**
¼ **teaspoon salt**
Freshly ground black pepper

Grated Romano cheese

Pasta Paella

Tradition is tampered with here in a delightful way that still captures the spirit of a classic Spanish paella but puts a pasta spin on it. Instead of Valencia rice, orzo pasta is used as the starchy base. The texture is somewhat different, but all the flavors and the impact remain. Be as indulgent as you'd like with the seafood. Shrimp can be joined with lobster, squid, or chunks of crab.

MAKES:
4 to 6 servings

PREP:
20 minutes

COOK:
40 minutes

1 tablespoon olive oil

6 to 8 ounces cured Spanish chorizo or linguica sausage, sliced

4 to 6 chicken thighs, skin removed

1 large onion, chopped

1 large red or green bell pepper, chopped

½ cup (2 ounces) diced smoked pork loin, well-smoked ham, or prosciutto

1 teaspoon paprika

½ teaspoon ground coriander

2 teaspoons sherry vinegar or red wine vinegar

2 large garlic cloves, minced

⅓ cup dry white wine

1 cup orzo

⅓ cup converted long-grain white rice

3 cups chicken stock or reduced-sodium canned broth

¼ teaspoon saffron threads or a pinch of ground saffron

2 bay leaves

½ teaspoon dried oregano

12 ounces peeled large shrimp

1 cup tiny frozen peas, thawed

1 medium tomato, diced

½ cup minced fresh parsley

Salt

Cayenne

1. In a large nonreactive sauté pan or Dutch oven, heat the olive oil over medium-high heat. Add the sausage and cook, stirring often, until it begins to brown, about 5 minutes. Add the chicken and continue to cook, turning, until both are well browned, 5 to 7 minutes. Set them aside and pour off all but 1 tablespoon of the fat from the pan.

2. Add the onion, bell pepper, pork, paprika, and coriander to the pan. Cook over high heat, stirring often, until the onion is softened, 6 to 8 minutes. Add the vinegar and stir up the browned bits from the bottom of the pan. Add the garlic and cook, stirring constantly, until fragrant, 30 seconds. Add the wine and cook until most of it has evaporated, about 2 minutes.

3. Stir in the pasta and rice. Cook, stirring, 1 minute; then add the chicken stock, saffron, bay leaves, and oregano. Bring to a boil and add the chicken. Reduce the heat to medium and simmer 5 minutes. Add the sausage and shrimp, cover, and cook until almost all of the liquid is absorbed, 8 to 11 minutes.

4. Add the peas and tomato, turn off the heat, and let stand 5 minutes. Add the parsley and season with salt and cayenne to taste. (Depending on the saltiness of the chicken stock and the sausage as well as the heat of the sausage, neither seasoning may be needed.) Remove and discard the bay leaves before serving.

Linguica is a mild, uncooked, smoked Portuguese sausage made from coarsely ground pork butts. Typically seasoned with garlic, cinnamon, pepper, salt, and cumin seeds, it's then cured in a vinegar pickling liquid before getting stuffed into a casing. Andouille, chorizo sausage, or tasso ham could be substituted for linguica if necessary, but these substitutes will provide a spicier taste.

The most expensive spice in the world actually costs more, ounce for ounce, than gold! **Saffron** is hand-harvested from the three stigmas of the tiny crocus flower in Spain; this painstaking task accounts for the high price. Saffron has a very delicate taste, but is highly aromatic. Especially popular in Indian cuisine such as curry and rice recipes, it is also used in paella, bouillabaisse, and risotto. Saffron is used to tint foods yellow, but the unsoaked strands are dark reddish-orange: the deeper their color, the higher the quality. Saffron powder is often doctored with non-saffron ingredients to increase profits, so it's advisable to buy only the threads.

Penne with White Beans, Chard & Anchovies

The juxtaposition here of the crisp, crunchy bread crumbs with tender greens, pasta, and beans is truly sensational. It is a classic Tuscan partnership that adds grace to any table.

MAKES:
3 to 4 servings

PREP:
10 minutes

COOK:
20 minutes

2 large garlic cloves

6 flat anchovies, patted dry

½ teaspoon crushed hot red pepper

½ cup olive oil

1 cup fresh bread crumbs

2 tablespoons finely minced fresh basil or 1 teaspoon dried

¼ teaspoon freshly ground black pepper

1 cup cooked or canned small white beans, such as navy beans

1 small plum tomato, seeded and finely diced

¾ teaspoon salt

12 ounces penne

1 bunch of red or green Swiss chard, stems trimmed and leaves cut into 1-inch ribbons

Grated Parmesan cheese

1 In a mini-chopper, mince the garlic, anchovies, and hot red pepper together. Or combine the same ingredients on a cutting board and chop and smash them together, using the flat side of a knife, to form a coarse paste. Set aside.

2 In a large pot, heat ¼ cup of the olive oil over medium-high heat. Add the bread crumbs and cook, stirring constantly, until crisp, 3 to 4 minutes. Stir in the basil and ⅛ teaspoon of the pepper. Transfer the bread crumb mixture to a small bowl, and set aside. Wipe out the pot with a paper towel.

3 Heat the remaining ¼ cup olive oil in the pot over medium heat. Add the garlic paste and cook, stirring constantly, until the garlic begins to soften, about 2 minutes. Add the beans, tomato, ¼ teaspoon of the salt, and the remaining ⅛ teaspoon pepper. Cook until heated through, 1 to 2 minutes. Transfer the bean mixture to a large bowl.

4 Partially fill the pot with water. Add the remaining ½ teaspoon salt and bring to a boil. Add the pasta and cook until almost tender, about 6 minutes. Add the Swiss chard and continue to cook until the pasta is tender but still firm, about 5 minutes longer. Drain thoroughly, shaking the colander to remove as much moisture as possible.

5 Add the pasta and chard to the bean mixture, and mix lightly. Top with the bread crumbs. Pass the Parmesan cheese separately.

The true **anchovy** comes only from the Mediterranean and southern European coastlines. These tiny saltwater fish, related to sardines, have an intense, briny taste. They're either filleted, salt-cured, or canned in oil, and sold flat or rolled. Anchovies packed in salt are sold in delicatessens; you must remove the bones before using the fish in recipes. Because they're so salty, anchovies are used sparingly. To lessen the saltiness, soak them in cool water for about 30 minutes, then drain them and pat dry with paper towels.

Parmesan cheese takes its name from the city of Parma in Italy, though it originated midway between that city and Reggio, where the finest Italian variety, Parmigiano-Reggiano, is produced. This hard, thick-crusted Italian cheese made from skimmed or partially skimmed cow's milk has a full, sharp, salty, flavor and granular texture—the result of up to two years of aging. Cheeses labeled *stravecchio* are three years old, while *stravecchiones* have been aged for four years. Buy Parmesan in block form, to grate fresh as needed.

Pasta Shells with Sausage in Tomato-Cream Sauce

Simple, rustic, and classically Italian, this dish can be prepared in short order. Shells are a good choice, but other similar types of noodles can be used.

MAKES:
3 to 4 servings

PREP:
10 minutes

COOK:
30 minutes

1	**pound medium pasta shells**
2	**tablespoons olive oil**
½	**pound mild Italian sausage in casing**
1½	**pounds plum tomatoes, peeled, seeded, and chopped**
2	**teaspoons chopped fresh rosemary or ½ teaspoon dried**
2	**teaspoons chopped fresh basil or ½ teaspoon dried**
1	**small garlic clove, minced**
	Crushed hot red pepper
½	**cup heavy cream**
½	**teaspoon salt**
⅓	**cup grated Parmesan cheese**

1 In a large pot, cook the pasta, according to package directions, until tender but still firm, about 10 minutes. Drain. Transfer the pasta to a large serving bowl or platter. Add 1 tablespoon of the olive oil and mix lightly to coat. Cover with foil to keep warm and set aside.

2 Place the sausages in the pot and add enough water to cover. Bring to a boil and cook 3 minutes. Drain the sausages and cut into ¼-inch-thick slices. Wipe out the pot with a paper towel and add the remaining 1 tablespoon olive oil. Place over medium-high heat and add the sausage. Cook, turning occasionally, until the sausage is nicely browned, 4 to 5 minutes. Drain off the excess fat.

3 Add the tomatoes, 1 teaspoon of the rosemary, 1 teaspoon of the basil, the garlic, and a dash of the hot red pepper to the pot. Cook over medium heat, stirring occasionally, 5 minutes. Add the cream and salt and continue to cook until the cream has reduced slightly, 5 to 7 minutes. Add the remaining 1 teaspoon rosemary and basil. Pour over the hot pasta and mix lightly to coat. Serve topped with the Parmesan cheese.

Andrew's Ready Spaghetti

This clever and simple dinner comes from the inquiring mind of a 10-year-old who wondered why spaghetti is cooked in water instead of sauce. Why, indeed? Here the pasta cooks right in the sauce, making an uncommonly easy meal. During tomato season, a few fresh diced tomatoes and a handful of chopped fresh basil make nice additions. Stir them into the pan after it has been removed from the heat.

MAKES:
3 to 4 servings
PREP:
5 minutes
COOK:
20 minutes
STAND:
5 minutes

1. In a large saucepan, combine the beef, onion, hot pepper, basil, and oregano. Cook, stirring often to break up any large lumps, until the meat is browned, 4 to 5 minutes.

2. Add 2½ cups water, the marinara sauce, and spaghetti and bring to a boil, stirring often. Cover, reduce the heat to low, and cook, stirring often, until the spaghetti is almost tender and most of the liquid is absorbed, 13 to 15 minutes.

3. Turn off the heat and let the pan stand, covered, 5 minutes. Season with pepper to taste and serve sprinkled with the cheese.

½ **pound ground beef or ground turkey**
1 **small onion, chopped**
Pinch of crushed hot red pepper
1 **teaspoon dried basil**
½ **teaspoon dried oregano**

1½ **cups marinara sauce**
12 **ounces spaghetti, broken in half**

Freshly ground pepper
1 **cup grated Parmesan cheese**

Seafood Pasta Primavera

This extravagant pairing of seasonal vegetables and shellfish was designed with romance in mind. But there's no reason not to double the recipe and extend the warmth to larger gatherings. For the grandest of occasions, add a sliced lobster tail to the mix.

MAKES:
2 servings

PREP:
20 minutes

COOK:
20 minutes

8 ounces trenette, pappardelle, or fettuccine

1½ tablespoons olive oil

1 large garlic clove, cut in half

1 medium shallot, minced

¼ cup dry vermouth or white wine
1½ tablespoons seasoned rice vinegar

8 ounces large or jumbo shrimp, peeled with the tail left intact and deveined

4 ounces bay scallops

2 ounces small wild mushrooms, such as porcini or shiitake, sliced in half

4 ounces slender asparagus, diagonally cut into 1-inch pieces

1 small orange or red bell pepper, finely diced

½ cup tiny frozen peas
½ cup heavy cream

1 small plum tomato, seeded and finely diced

3 to 4 tablespoons mixed minced fresh herbs, such as tarragon, dill, and basil

¼ teaspoon salt
¼ teaspoon freshly ground pepper

¼ cup grated Parmesan cheese

1 In a large pot, cook the pasta, according to package directions, until tender but still firm, about 10 minutes. Drain. Transfer the pasta to a medium bowl. Add ½ tablespoon of the olive oil and mix lightly to coat. Cover with foil to keep warm, and set aside.

2 Heat the remaining 1 tablespoon olive oil with the garlic in the pot over medium-high heat. Remove and discard the garlic when it starts to sizzle, about 1 minute. Add the shallot to the pan and cook, stirring occasionally, until it begins to soften, about 2 minutes.

3 Increase the heat to high. Add the vermouth and the vinegar and heat to a simmer. Add the shrimp, scallops, mushrooms, asparagus, and bell pepper and cook, stirring often, until the seafood is opaque throughout, 3 to 4 minutes.

4 Stir in the peas and cream and simmer until the sauce thickens slightly, 2 to 3 minutes. Remove the pot from the heat and add the tomato, herbs, salt, and pepper. To serve, divide the pasta between 2 serving plates and top with the sauce and Parmesan cheese.

The Italian phrase **_primavera_** means "spring style," and it refers to the use of raw or blanched fresh vegetables. One of the most popular dishes prepared in this manner is pasta primavera, where the pasta gets tossed or topped with diced or julienned cooked vegetables.

Trenette is a similar noodle to tagliatelle, long but thicker and narrower. **Pappardelle** are wide, flat ribbons of pasta with rippled sides.

Tortellini with Sausage & Pepper Ragout

*Fresh, filled pastas adapt perfectly to cooking right in a sauce,
making them a great one-pot, one-step option. Most supermarkets sell several
shapes and flavors of filled pasta. Cheese- or spinach-filled is a good choice here.*

MAKES:
2 to 3 servings
PREP:
10 minutes
COOK:
20 minutes

1	tablespoon olive oil
6	ounces cooked chicken or turkey sausage, sliced 1½ inches thick
1	small onion, diced
1	small red or green bell pepper, cut into ¾-inch squares

1½	cups marinara sauce
1	teaspoon dried basil
½	teaspoon dried oregano
	Pinch of crushed hot red pepper

12	ounces fresh or thawed frozen tortellini or cappelletti

¼	cup grated Parmesan cheese

1 In a large saucepan, heat the olive oil over medium-high heat. Add the sausage, onion, and bell pepper and cook, stirring often, until the sausage is browned and the pepper has softened slightly, 4 to 5 minutes. Add the marinara sauce, basil, oregano, hot red pepper, and 1 cup water. Bring to a boil.

2 Add the tortellini, reduce the heat to low, and simmer, uncovered, 15 minutes, stirring often, until the pasta is tender but still firm. Serve sprinkled with the Parmesan cheese.

Baked Tortellini

The time to start thinking about this dish is when the nights turn chilly, and heartier fare is requested.

MAKES:
8 servings

PREP:
15 minutes

COOK:
55 minutes

1 Preheat the oven to 350° F. In a large flameproof casserole, cook the pasta according to package directions until tender but still firm, about 5 minutes. Drain. Rinse the pasta under cold running water and drain again.

2 Cook the sausage in the casserole with ½ inch of water over medium heat, turning, until no longer pink in the center, 4 to 5 minutes. Prick the sausage in several places with a sharp knife; drain off the water. Return the sausage to the casserole and cook over medium heat, turning, until the sausage is browned, 4 to 6 minutes. Cut the sausage into ½-inch-thick slices, and set aside.

3 Return the casserole to medium-high heat. Add the vinegar and stir up the browned bits from the bottom of the pan. Add the onions, bell pepper, zucchini, and hot red pepper and cook, stirring often, until the onions are softened, 6 to 7 minutes. Remove the pan from the heat and mix in the tomatoes, tomato sauce, sausage, and tortellini.

4 In a medium bowl, combine the mozzarella, fontina, and Parmesan cheeses and the basil, and mix lightly. Stir 1 cup of the cheese mixture into the pasta in the casserole and sprinkle the remaining cheese mixture on top. Transfer to the oven and bake 35 minutes, or until heated through.

3 **(9-ounce) packages fresh tortellini**

12 **ounces hot or mild Italian sausage in casing**

1 **tablespoon balsamic vinegar**

2 **medium onions, chopped**
1 **large red bell pepper, chopped**
1 **medium zucchini, chopped**
½ **teaspoon crushed hot red pepper**

1 **(14½-ounce) can diced tomatoes, well drained**
1 **(15-ounce) container plum tomato sauce or marinara sauce**

1 **cup shredded mozzarella cheese**
1 **cup shredded fontina cheese**
1 **cup shredded Parmesan cheese**
½ **cup minced fresh basil**

Pasta & Pepper Frittata

*Pasta may not be the most typical addition to frittata, but it turns the delicate
egg dish into a hearty meal. In this rendition, a colorful
mix of peppers are cooked along with lots of onion, garlic, and a little nip
of hot pepper, and then bound with eggs, cheese, and pasta.*

MAKES:
6 to 8 servings

PREP:
20 minutes

COOK:
20 minutes

STAND:
10 minutes

¼ cup olive oil

3 large red bell peppers, cut into
¾-inch squares

2 medium green bell peppers, cut into
¾-inch squares

1 medium onion, finely chopped

3 large garlic cloves, minced

1 jalapeño or serrano pepper,
seeded and minced

4 sun-dried tomato halves, minced

1 teaspoon dried basil

1 teaspoon salt

1 teaspoon balsamic vinegar

¼ teaspoon freshly ground pepper

6 ounces cooked vermicelli or thin spaghetti

8 eggs

¾ cup shredded provolone cheese

½ cup grated Parmesan cheese

1 Preheat the oven to 350° F. In a deep ovenproof casserole or skillet, heat the olive oil over high heat. Add the bell peppers, onion, garlic, jalapeño pepper, sun-dried tomatoes, basil, and ½ teaspoon of the salt. Cook, stirring often, until the peppers are tender, 8 to 10 minutes. Stir in the vinegar and ⅛ teaspoon of the pepper. Add the pasta and toss lightly. Cook 1 minute.

2 In a medium bowl, whisk the eggs with the remaining ½ teaspoon salt and ⅛ teaspoon pepper. Stir in the provolone cheese. Pour the egg mixture over the vegetable mixture in the pan; tilt the pan to distribute evenly. Cook over medium heat until the eggs begin to set, 2 to 3 minutes. Top with the Parmesan cheese and transfer to the oven.

3 Bake 8 to 10 minutes, or just until the frittata is set in the center. Remove the pan from the oven and let stand 10 minutes. Carefully loosen the frittata from the sides of the pan. Cut into wedges and serve hot or at room temperature.

Unlike an omelet, the Italian **frittata** usually has its ingredients mixed in with the eggs rather than being folded inside. It can be flipped during preparation, or the top might finish cooking under a broiling unit. A frittata has a firmer consistency because it's cooked very slowly over low heat.

A centuries-old specialty of Modena, Italy, **balsamic vinegar** is made from reduced white Trebbiano grape juice. Its dark color and pungent sweetness come from aging in barrels—of various woods and in gradually diminishing sizes—over a period of years. This results in thick, tartly sweet, and intensely aromatic vinegar.

Eating habits constantly evolve to reflect new experiences, different sensibilities, acquired tastes, and shifts in attitudes. One of the changes gaining momentum is the burgeoning interest in meatless and mostly meatless meals. Vegetarianism as a lifestyle continues to grow, but so, too, does a broader outlook on eating habits that embraces occasional forays into meatless meals. If meat was once the defining aspect of a balanced meal, we now know that other foods can ably and interestingly stand in its place. There are seemingly endless choices that go well beyond the predictable meat-and-potatoes duet, so that even those who once were skeptical about meatless meals have discovered that meatless doesn't mean weird, mundane, or unsatisfying.

Mostly Meatless Meals

Peppery Chickpea & Okra Stew, Fragrant Red Lentils & Jasmine Rice with Fried Onions, and **Pony's Cowpoke Pintos** admirably show how well dried beans and legumes can take the place of meat. These foods are healthful and very inexpensive. Dried beans that are soaked and cooked are the very best option, but canned allows for the serendipity of last-minute menu planning. Increasingly, the produce department of many supermarkets stocks packages of dried beans that have been soaked and partially cooked. These can be table-ready in about 15 minutes—a terrific convenience.

Grains and rice also offer delicious possibilities. The colorful **Carrot Couscous with Ragout of Spring Vegetables**; **Punjab-Spiced Eggplant, Millet & Potato Stew**; and **Rice Torte with Creamy Eggplant & Mushrooms** are delicious forays into the world of grains.

If you are not a vegetarian, very small amounts of meat can be used to flavor vegetables, pasta, and grains, a trick that other cuisines have relied on for centuries, and people are now eagerly adapting to suit their tastes. This tactic is used in the **Bean Stew with Cabbage & Radicchio**; **Risotto with Asparagus, Mushrooms & Smoked Trout**; and **Bleu Black Eyes with Spinach & Bacon**.

Aztec Vegetable Stew with Black Beans & Corn

A full palette of colors, flavors, and textures are the hallmarks of this dish. It's an ideal recipe to make in early autumn, when winter squash's season overlaps with the late summer harvest. Because the squash is peeled before it's cooked, butternut is the best choice since its smooth shape makes the skin easy to remove. Be sure to cut the flesh into small cubes so it cooks right in step with the other vegetables.

MAKES:
4 servings
PREP:
30 minutes
COOK:
15 minutes

1 In a large skillet, heat the oil over medium–high heat. Add the onion, garlic, and squash. Cook, stirring often, until the squash begins to soften, about 5 minutes.

2 Reduce the heat to medium. Add the poblano pepper, bell pepper, zucchini, cumin, orange zest, and salt. Cook, stirring occasionally, until the squash and peppers are tender, 4 to 5 minutes.

3 Add the corn, beans, and tomatoes and cook until heated through, about 3 minutes. Add the cilantro, cayenne, and additional salt to taste. Serve hot or at room temperature.

2	tablespoons vegetable oil
1	medium onion, chopped
1	large garlic clove, minced
1¼	cups butternut squash, peeled and cut into ½-inch cubes
1	poblano pepper, finely diced
1	red bell pepper, diced
2	medium zucchini, diced
½	teaspoon ground cumin
½	teaspoon grated orange zest
½	teaspoon salt
1	cup corn kernels
1	(16-ounce) can black beans, rinsed and drained
3	small tomatoes, diced
½	cup chopped cilantro
⅛ to ¼	teaspoon cayenne, to taste

Bean Stew with Cabbage & Radicchio

*Wintry and warming, this simple dish is best served
with hot bread, spread with tangy goat cheese.*

MAKES:
4 servings

SOAK:
12 hours or
overnight

PREP:
15 minutes

COOK:
1 hour, 45
minutes

¼ **pound pancetta or thick-sliced bacon,
finely diced**

1 **medium onion, chopped**

1½ **cups Great Northern beans, soaked 12 hours
or overnight**

3 **cups vegetable stock, chicken stock, or
reduced-sodium canned broth**

2 **sprigs of fresh rosemary or 1 teaspoon dried**

1 **teaspoon coarsely ground black pepper**

½ **of a small head of Savoy or green cabbage,
cut into 1-inch chunks**

1 **large head of radicchio, cut into
1-inch chunks**

¼ **cup chopped fresh basil leaves**

2 **teaspoons balsamic or red wine vinegar**

½ **teaspoon salt**

¼ **cup grated Parmesan cheese**

1 In a large, heavy pot, cook the pancetta over medium heat until it begins to render some of its fat, about 5 minutes. Add the onion and continue to cook, stirring occasionally, until the pancetta is crisp, 7 to 8 minutes.

2 Add the beans, vegetable stock, rosemary, and pepper. Bring to a boil, reduce the heat to medium-low, and simmer, partially covered, until the beans are almost tender, about 1¼ hours.

3 Add the cabbage and radicchio. Continue to cook until the beans and vegetables are tender, 12 to 15 minutes longer. Remove from the heat and stir in the basil, vinegar, and salt. Serve sprinkled with the Parmesan cheese.

Carrot Couscous with Ragout of Spring Vegetables

Fresh carrot juice, used to soften the couscous, imparts a tawny golden hue and subtle sweetness. It is increasingly available in produce departments or health food stores, or use canned carrot juice as an alternative.

MAKES:
3 to 4 servings

PREP:
20 minutes

COOK:
15 minutes

1. Bring the carrot juice to a boil. Pour over the couscous in a medium heatproof bowl, cover tightly, and let stand 10 minutes.

2. Meanwhile, heat 2 tablespoons of the olive oil in a large nonstick skillet over high heat. Add the onion, asparagus, and bell pepper. Cook, stirring often, until the vegetables begin to brown at the edges, 6 to 8 minutes.

3. Add the morels and cook just until they are heated through, 1 minute. Add the cream, mustard and ¼ teaspoon of the salt. Cook, stirring constantly, until the cream coats the vegetables, about 1 minute. Remove from the heat and stir in the basil.

4. Fluff the couscous with a fork and add the remaining 1 tablespoon olive oil and ½ teaspoon salt, the curry powder, spinach, and mint. Mix well. Mound on a platter, top with the vegetable mixture, and serve.

¾	cup carrot juice plus 2 tablespoons
1	cup couscous
3	tablespoons olive oil
1	small Vidalia or other sweet onion, finely diced
½	pound slender asparagus, trimmed and diagonally cut into 1-inch pieces
1	small red bell pepper, finely diced
¼	pound morels, cremini, or other wild mushrooms, quartered
3	tablespoons heavy cream
½	teaspoon Dijon mustard
¾	teaspoon salt
1	tablespoon minced fresh basil
¼	teaspoon curry powder
1½	cups minced tender young spinach leaves
2	teaspoons minced fresh mint, if available

Punjab-Spiced Eggplant, Millet & Potato Stew

In Indian cooking, potatoes and eggplant are frequently joined together in the stew pot. Simmered with spices and aromatics, these two ingredients harmonize in taste and texture. The surprise addition here is millet, little bits of grain with an agreeable crunch and a subtle, nutty taste.

MAKES:
3 to 4 servings

PREP:
20 minutes

COOK:
25 minutes

1 tablespoon vegetable oil

½ teaspoon cumin seeds

½ teaspoon mustard seeds

¼ teaspoon ground cardamom

1 serrano pepper, minced

1 garlic clove, minced

1 piece of fresh ginger (about a ¾-inch cube), minced

¼ cup millet

3 Japanese or very slender young eggplants, cut into ¾-inch dice

2 medium yellow potatoes, scrubbed and cut into ¾-inch dice

1 cup vegetable stock or reduced-sodium canned broth

1 tablespoon brown sugar

¼ teaspoon salt

½ cup tiny frozen peas, thawed

3 tablespoons minced cilantro

1 tablespoon minced fresh mint

1 In a large skillet, heat the oil with the cumin seeds, mustard seeds, and cardamom over high heat. When the mustard seeds begin to pop, after 1 to 2 minutes, add the serrano pepper, garlic, and ginger and cook, stirring constantly, 1 minute.

2 Add the millet, reduce the heat to medium, and cook until the millet is lightly toasted, 3 to 4 minutes. Add the eggplant and potatoes, and mix well. Stir in the vegetable stock, brown sugar, and salt.

3 Cover and cook over medium-low heat until the potatoes are tender, about 20 minutes. Add the peas and cook 1 minute longer. Remove the skillet from the heat, stir in the cilantro and mint, and serve.

Madras-Spiced Lentils with Spinach

Lentils, packed with protein and loaded with rustic character, have a humble appeal that is well suited to casual meals. Indian cooking uses them in countless ways, often combining them with potatoes and spinach and the heady perfume of spices.

MAKES:
4 to 6 servings

PREP:
20 minutes

COOK:
25 minutes

1 In a large saucepan, heat the oil over medium-high heat. Add the curry powder, cumin seeds, cardamom, turmeric, and cayenne and cook, stirring constantly, 1 minute. Add the onion, garlic, and ginger. Cook, stirring often, until the onion begins to soften, 3 to 4 minutes.

2 Add the lentils, potatoes, stock, and salt, cover, and bring to a boil. Reduce the heat to medium-low and simmer gently until the lentils are just tender, 18 to 20 minutes.

3 Add the spinach, cilantro, mint, and butter, stir well, and remove from the heat. Sprinkle with the tomato just before serving.

2 tablespoons vegetable oil
1 tablespoon curry powder
1 teaspoon cumin seeds
½ teaspoon cardamom
½ teaspoon turmeric
½ teaspoon cayenne

1 large onion, chopped
2 large garlic cloves, minced
1 piece of fresh ginger (about a ¾-inch cube), minced

1⅓ cups brown or green lentils
2 small red potatoes, scrubbed and cut into ½-inch dice
4 cups vegetable stock or water
1 teaspoon salt

1 pound fresh spinach, coarsely chopped
1 cup chopped cilantro
¼ cup chopped fresh mint
1 tablespoon unsalted butter

1 medium tomato, diced

Peppery Chickpea & Okra Stew

Arabian and African influences glimmer in this richly spiced stew that is emboldened with a hefty kick of cayenne. Recognizing that people have different attitudes about okra, there are two routes that can be taken. As the recipe is written, the okra cooks to a soft and, some would say, slippery texture. For those who prefer okra to be served crisp, it can be added much later in the cooking time.

MAKES:
6 to 8 servings

SOAK:
12 hours or overnight

PREP:
15 minutes

COOK:
1 hour, 45 minutes

5   tablespoons olive oil

1   pound okra, trimmed and halved crosswise

1   teaspoon ground coriander

1¼   teaspoons salt

1   large onion, chopped

4   large garlic cloves, minced

2   (14½-ounce) cans diced tomatoes, juices reserved

4   cups vegetable stock or water

¾ to 1   teaspoon cayenne

1   pound chickpeas, soaked 12 hours or overnight

1   piece of fresh ginger (about a ¾-inch cube), minced

1   tablespoon peanut butter

1   tablespoon wine vinegar or sherry vinegar

1 In a large soup pot, heat 3 tablespoons of the olive oil over high heat. Add the okra and season with the coriander and ¼ teaspoon of the salt. Cook, shaking the pan often, until the okra turns bright green and begins to soften, 4 to 5 minutes. Remove from the pan and set aside.

2 Heat the remaining 2 tablespoons olive oil in the same pot over high heat. Add the onion and cook, stirring often, until it begins to brown, 5 minutes. Add the garlic and cook, stirring often, 2 minutes. Add the tomatoes with their juices, the vegetable stock, cayenne, and drained chickpeas. Cover and cook gently 1 hour.

3 Add the okra, ginger, peanut butter, and remaining 1 teaspoon salt. Mix well. Cook, uncovered, until the beans are softened, about 30 minutes. Stir in the vinegar and serve.

Although it's also called red pepper, don't confuse **cayenne** with red peppercorns. The chili peppers used in this pungent powder were originally grown in the Cayenne region of French Guyana. Though the same peppers are now grown in India, Japan, and Africa, the name cayenne has stuck. Unlike its milder cousins, cayenne pepper uses the chili's seeds and membranes, which store the heat, making it especially fiery. This sizzle acts as a great foil to rich ingredients. Cayenne preparations vary by producer, so flavor and color will vary.

Fragrant Red Lentils & Jasmine Rice with Fried Onions

Lentils and rice frequently are paired together, with good reason—they complement each other tastewise as well as nutritionally. Mixed with a bouquet of spices, then topped with crisp onions, they make a great meatless main course offering.

MAKES:
4 to 6 servings

PREP:
10 minutes

COOK:
25 minutes

STAND:
5 minutes

⅔   **cup red lentils**

½   **teaspoon cumin seeds**

1   **cinnamon stick, broken in half**

4   **whole green cardamom pods or ¼ teaspoon ground cardamom**

2   **tablespoons vegetable oil**

1   **large onion, halved crosswise and cut into wedges**

2   **teaspoons chutney**

1⅓   **cups jasmine or basmati rice**

2⅔   **cups vegetable stock, chicken stock, or reduced-sodium canned broth**

3   **bay leaves**

1   **jalapeño or serrano pepper, minced**

¾   **teaspoon salt**

⅓   **cup chopped cilantro**

1   **cup plain yogurt**

1   In a large, heavy skillet, combine the lentils, cumin, cinnamon stick, and cardamom. Cook over high heat, stirring often, until the lentils begin to brown, about 5 minutes. Remove from the pan and set aside.

2   Heat the oil in the same pan. Add the onion and cook, stirring often, until the onions are softened and have begun to brown at the edges, 6 to 8 minutes. Transfer half of the onions to a small bowl, stir in the chutney, and set aside. Leave the remaining onions in the pan.

3   Add the rice, vegetable stock, bay leaves, hot pepper, and salt to the onions in the pan. Cover and bring to a boil. Reduce the heat to medium-low and simmer gently 5 minutes. Add the lentils, cover, and continue to cook until the lentils and rice are tender, 8 to 11 minutes. Remove from the heat and let stand, covered, 5 minutes. Remove and discard the bay leaves and cardamom pods. Add the reserved onions and cilantro. Serve topped with dollops of yogurt.

Potato & Onion Stew

Adapted from an old French country recipe, this is a testament to the charms of a simple table. It asks for nothing more than lots of bread, a lusty bottle of wine, and good company.

1 In a large heavy saucepan, cook the salt pork over medium heat until it is crisp and has rendered most of its fat, about 8 minutes. Add the onions and cook, stirring occasionally, until they begin to soften, 3 to 5 minutes.

2 Sprinkle on the flour, add the bay leaves and thyme, and increase the heat to high. Pour in the wine and stir up any browned bits from the bottom of the pan. Cook until the wine has almost completely evaporated, 2 to 3 minutes.

3 Add the potatoes, vegetable stock, and pepper, cover, and bring to a boil. Reduce the heat to medium-low and simmer until the potatoes are very tender, 50 to 60 minutes.

4 Sprinkle with the paprika and chives and season with additional pepper to taste. Remove and discard the bay leaves before serving.

¼	pound salt pork, well rinsed and cut into 1 x ¼-inch strips
2	medium onions, cut into 1-inch chunks
1½	tablespoons flour
4	large bay leaves
1	teaspoon dried thyme leaves
¼	cup dry white wine or vermouth
2	pounds potatoes, including a mix of yellow, small red, and Idaho, scrubbed and cut into large chunks
2	cups vegetable stock or water
¼	teaspoon freshly ground pepper
	Hungarian sweet paprika
2	tablespoons minced fresh chives

MAKES:
3 to 4 servings
PREP:
20 minutes
COOK:
1 hour, 5 minutes

Ratatouille with Poached Eggs

The summer harvest offers a garden of delights, among them eggplant, peppers, tomatoes, and summer squash. Classic French Provençal cooking ingeniously combined them into a long-simmered stew that can be used in so many ways. A topping of poached eggs and a bit of cheese is but one of many tasty options.

MAKES:
4 servings

PREP:
30 minutes

DRAIN:
30 minutes

COOK:
1 hour,
10 minutes

1   large eggplant, peeled and cut
    into ¾-inch cubes

    Salt

¼   cup olive oil

1   large onion, chopped

2   medium garlic cloves, minced

2   small zucchini, sliced ½ inch thick

1   small yellow squash, sliced ½ inch thick

1   small red bell pepper, diced

1   small green bell pepper, diced

4   plum tomatoes, diced

½   cup marinara sauce or tomato sauce

2   tablespoons minced fresh basil
    or 1¼ teaspoons dried

2   teaspoons minced fresh thyme leaves
    or ½ teaspoon dried

    Freshly ground black pepper

4   eggs

    Grated Parmesan cheese

1 Place the eggplant in a colander, sprinkle with salt, and toss lightly to coat. Let drain for 30 minutes. Wrap handfuls in a double thickness of paper towels, and squeeze dry. Set aside.

2 In a large flameproof casserole or saucepan, heat the oil over medium-high heat. Add the onion and garlic. Cook, stirring occasionally, until the onion is softened, 3 to 5 minutes.

3 Add the eggplant and cook, stirring, 3 minutes. Add the zucchini, yellow squash, bell peppers, tomatoes, marinara sauce, basil, thyme, ½ teaspoon salt, and black pepper to taste. Reduce the heat to low, cover, and simmer very gently until the vegetables are soft, about 1 hour.

4 Make four equally spaced wells in the vegetable mixture and carefully crack an egg into each. Cover the pan and cook until the eggs are set as desired, 4 to 5 minutes. Sprinkle with the Parmesan cheese, and serve at once.

Ratatouille Boats
with Goat Cheese, Olives & Capers

Ratatouille is one of the most versatile of vegetable stews, a hearty assemblage of the summer harvest that can be parlayed into many meals of differing styles. Nestling it into crisped bread shells and adding a pungent edge with olives and goat cheese is just one way to turn it into a terrific main course.

MAKES:
4 servings

PREP:
none to 2 hours

COOK:
15 minutes

1 If the ratatouille has been made ahead of time, gently reheat it. Place the broiler rack about 8 inches from the heat source and preheat the broiler.

2 Slice off the tops from the rolls and scoop out the soft bread from inside, leaving a ½- to ¾-inch-thick shell. Brush the inside of each shell with olive oil, paying particular attention to the upper edges. Broil until they are warmed and lightly toasted, 2 to 3 minutes, watching carefully so they don't burn.

3 Stir the olives, vinegar, capers, and all but ¼ cup of the goat cheese into the ratatouille. Divide the ratatouille mixture among the 4 bread shells and sprinkle the remaining cheese on top. Place under the broiler briefly, just until the cheese begins to bubble, about 2 minutes. Serve hot or at room temperature.

1 recipe Ratatouille with Poached Eggs (from page 164), omitting the eggs and Parmesan cheese

4 miniature round bread loaves or large hard rolls, about 8 ounces each
1 tablespoon olive oil

¼ cup Niçoise or other imported black olives
1 tablespoon balsamic or red wine vinegar
1 tablespoon drained capers
1 cup crumbled goat cheese (about 4 ounces)

Winter Squash with Hominy & Chilies

An abundant gift of organically grown butternut squash from Broadland Farms in Illinois prompted this recipe. It is a simple, meatless dish that simmers quietly into an explosion of vibrant colors and tastes.

MAKES:
4 servings

PREP:
20 minutes

COOK:
30 minutes

2 tablespoons unsalted butter

1 small butternut squash (about 1 pound), peeled, seeded, and cut into ¾-inch cubes

1 medium onion, chopped

1 large garlic clove, minced

1 small red bell pepper, chopped

1 small poblano or Anaheim pepper, diced

½ teaspoon salt

½ teaspoon dried sage

1 tablespoon pure ground red chili or chili powder

1 (29-ounce) can hominy, drained and rinsed

2 cups vegetable stock or broth

1 tablespoon flour

¼ cup heavy cream

¼ cup minced cilantro

1 In a large skillet, melt the butter over medium-high heat. Add the squash, onion, and garlic. Cook, stirring often, 5 minutes. Add the bell pepper, poblano pepper, salt, sage, and ground red chili, mix well, and cook 2 to 3 minutes longer.

2 Add the hominy and all but 1 tablespoon of the vegetable stock. Cover, reduce the heat to low, and simmer gently until the squash is tender, 20 to 25 minutes.

3 In a small bowl, blend the flour with the reserved 1 tablespoon broth to make a smooth paste. Stir into the pan along with the cream and cilantro. Cook 1 minute longer, then serve.

Red Chili Rice & Lentil Pilaf

Dried ancho chili peppers impart a deep red tint and a complex blend of flavorful heat to the pilaf. One chili will make a mildly piquant dish, while two will kick up the heat a bit. Stirring in some cream at serving time softens and unifies the flavors, but for a leaner finish, it can be left out.

MAKES:
4 servings

PREP:
5 minutes

SOAK:
20 minutes

COOK:
30 minutes

STAND:
5 minutes

1 Place the chili peppers in a small heatproof bowl and cover with ½ cup boiling water. Let stand 20 minutes. Drain and remove the stems and seeds. Place the peppers in a blender or food processor with ¾ cup of the vegetable stock and the garlic, and puree until smooth.

2 Cut the onion in half lengthwise. Cut one half into thin slivers and dice the other half. In a large saucepan, heat 1 tablespoon oil over medium-high heat. Add the onion slivers and cook, stirring, until they begin to brown at the edges, 4 to 5 minutes. Remove from the pan and set aside.

3 Heat the remaining 1 tablespoon oil in the same pan. Add the diced onion and cook, stirring often, until it begins to soften, 3 to 4 minutes. Add the rice and cook 1 minute longer. Add the lentils, cumin, salt, ancho puree, and remaining 2¼ cups vegetable stock. Cover and bring to a boil.

4 Reduce the heat to medium-low and simmer gently until the liquid is absorbed and the rice and lentils are tender, 20 minutes. Stir in the cream and let stand, covered, 5 minutes. Stir in the cilantro, top with the cheese, pepitas, and slivered onion, and serve.

1 to 2	ancho chilies
3	cups vegetable stock or reduced-sodium canned broth
1	large garlic clove, cut into thirds
1	medium onion
2	tablespoons vegetable oil
1	cup converted long-grain white rice
½	cup brown or green lentils
1	teaspoon ground cumin
½	teaspoon salt
½	cup heavy cream
½	cup minced cilantro
½	cup crumbled añejo or Romano cheese
½	cup pepitas (optional)

Malaysian Vegetable Stew with Gingery Coconut Milk

Exotic and heady with the complex aroma of sweet and hot flavors, this hearty stew is built around several root vegetables, including boniato, a Latin American root with a beguiling, sweet taste. If boniatos are not available, try parsnips or white potatoes instead.

MAKES:
6 servings

PREP:
45 minutes

COOK:
35 minutes

3	tablespoons vegetable oil
½	teaspoon cayenne
½	teaspoon cinnamon
¼	teaspoon ground cloves

2	large onions, coarsely chopped

1	tablespoon minced fresh ginger
2	large garlic cloves, minced
2	large jalapeño or serrano peppers, minced
3	tablespoons curry powder

4½	cups vegetable or chicken stock or reduced-sodium canned broth
4	large sweet potatoes, scrubbed and cut into chunks
2	medium boniatos, peeled and cut into ¾-inch chunks
2	medium turnips, peeled and cut into ¾-inch chunks
2	medium carrots, peeled and cut into ¾-inch chunks

1	yellow bell pepper, diced
1	red bell pepper, diced
2	medium zucchini, sliced 1 inch thick

1	cup unsweetened coconut milk
½	teaspoon salt

¼	cup chopped cilantro
2	scallions, sliced

1 In a large soup pot or flameproof casserole, heat the oil with the cayenne, cinnamon, and cloves. When it is hot, add the onions and cook, stirring often, until the onions begin to soften, 4 to 5 minutes. Add the ginger, garlic, jalapeño peppers, and curry powder and cook, stirring constantly, 1 minute.

2 Add 3½ cups of the vegetable stock, the sweet potatoes, boniatos, turnips, and carrots, cover, and bring to a boil. Reduce the heat to low and simmer gently until the vegetables are almost tender, 20 to 25 minutes.

3 Add the bell peppers, zucchini, and more vegetable stock if needed. Cook until all the vegetables are tender, 8 to 10 minutes. Add the coconut milk and salt and heat through. Stir in the cilantro and sprinkle the scallions on top.

Also known as a Cuban sweet potato, **boniato** stands out with its white flesh rather than the yellow or orange meat of other varieties. Boniatos tend to grow large, have an irregular shape, and the skin color varies from reddish to cream colored. They are drier, fluffier, and not as sweet as other sweet potatoes, with a flavor like that of roasted chestnuts. Look for them in Latin markets. Although available year round, there may be a scarcity during February and March.

Carbonnade of Root Vegetables

Carbonnade is a Flemish beef stew that relies on sweet caramelized onions and beer for its characteristic taste. This partnership is way too successful to limit just to meat. Here, root vegetables are similarly seasoned.

MAKES:
6 servings

PREP:
30 minutes

COOK:
1 hour

6	thick bacon slices, diced
3	medium onions, cut into 1-inch dice
1	teaspoon dried thyme leaves
1½	tablespoons balsamic or red wine vinegar
2	medium turnips, peeled and cut into 1-inch cubes
1	small rutabaga, peeled and cut into 1-inch cubes
1	small butternut squash, peeled, seeded, and cut into 1-inch cubes
2	medium yellow or red potatoes, scrubbed and cut into 1-inch cubes
3	medium carrots, peeled and cut into 1-inch lengths
2	tablespoons flour
¾	cup beer, preferably ale
¼	cup vegetable or chicken stock or reduced-sodium canned broth
1½	teaspoons brown sugar
1	teaspoon salt
¼	teaspoon grated nutmeg
½	teaspoon freshly ground pepper
1	teaspoon Dijon mustard
¼	cup minced parsley
½	cup grated Parmesan cheese

1 Preheat the oven to 350° F. In a large flameproof casserole, cook the bacon over medium heat until it is crisp. Drain off all but 3 tablespoons of the fat. Add the onions and thyme and cook, stirring occasionally, until the onions are very soft and begin to color, 10 to 12 minutes. Add 1 tablespoon vinegar and stir up any browned bits from the bottom of the pan.

2 Add the remaining vegetables and the flour to the casserole, stirring so the flour dissolves. Stir in the beer, vegetable stock, brown sugar, salt, nutmeg, and pepper. Cover, transfer to the oven, and bake 45 to 55 minutes, or until the vegetables are tender. Stir in the mustard, parsley, and remaining ½ tablespoon vinegar. Serve sprinkled with the cheese.

Bleu Black Eyes with Spinach & Bacon

Sassy and southern, this dish has a trio of bold flavors supporting the black-eyed peas. Quick-cooking black eyes are sold in many produce departments. Soaked and precooked, they are tender and table-ready in 15 minutes.

MAKES:
4 servings
PREP:
15 minutes
COOK:
20 minutes

1 In a large saucepan of boiling water, cook the peas until they are tender, about 12 minutes. Remove to a colander to drain and set aside.

2 Combine the bacon and the hot peppers in the same pan and cook, stirring occasionally, over medium heat until the bacon begins to give off some fat. Add the onion and bell pepper. Continue to cook until the onion begins to brown, about 5 minutes.

3 Add the black-eyed peas, walnut oil, vinegar, salt, and black pepper and cook just until hot, 1 minute. The mixture should be peppery. Add the cilantro.

4 Serve hot or at room temperature, with the black eyes spooned atop a bed of spinach and garnished with the crumbled cheese.

1	(12-ounce) package quick-cooking black-eyed peas
3	thick slices of bacon, diced
2	small dried hot red peppers
1	medium sweet onion, such as Vidalia or Maui, diced
1	medium red bell pepper, diced
2	tablespoons walnut oil or olive oil
2	tablespoons cider vinegar
1/4	teaspoon salt
1/4	teaspoon freshly ground black pepper
1/2	cup minced cilantro or parsley
6 to 8	ounces salad spinach, washed and dried
1/4	cup (1 ounce) crumbled bleu cheese

Pony's Cowpoke Pintos

MAKES:
6 to 8 servings

SOAK:
12 hours or
overnight

PREP:
10 minutes

COOK:
1 hour,
40 minutes

A big pan of cornbread and ice cold beer turns these cowboy beans into a fun-time feast. Great as a main course, the beans are also an appropriate side-dish for picnics and barbecues.

5   bacon slices, preferably applewood-smoked, diced

1   large onion, chopped

3   garlic cloves, minced

2   jalapeño peppers, thinly sliced

2   tablespoons chili powder

1   tablespoon ground cumin

2   cups dried pinto beans, soaked 12 hours or overnight

1   (14½-ounce) can diced tomatoes, juices reserved

1   cup beer

½   cup barbecue sauce

¾   teaspoon salt

1 In a large saucepan, cook the bacon over medium heat until it is crisp, about 5 minutes. Add the onion, garlic, and jalapeño peppers. Cook, stirring often, until the onion begins to soften, 4 to 5 minutes.

2 Stir in the chili powder and cumin, and then add the drained beans, the tomatoes with their juices, beer, 1 cup water, barbecue sauce, and salt.

3 Cover partially and bring to a boil. Reduce the heat to medium-low and simmer gently until the beans are tender, about 1½ hours, stirring the mixture often and adding additional water if the mixture seems too dry.

Arugula & Roasted Pepper Frittata with Fresh Mozzarella

This makes a lovely presentation, with the vibrant red and green vegetables dramatically accented by the soft, melting white cheese. Unlike omelets, to which they're closely related, frittatas require neither a deft hand at flipping them nor an absolute last-minute cooking.

MAKES:
4 to 6 servings

PREP:
10 minutes

COOK:
15 minutes

1. Preheat the broiler. In a 10-inch ovenproof skillet or gratin pan, heat 1 tablespoon of the olive oil over high heat. Add the bell pepper and cook 1 minute. Add the arugula and stir over high heat just until it wilts, about 30 seconds. Add the vinegar, a dash of the salt, and a dash of black pepper. Remove from the skillet and set aside.

2. In a medium mixing bowl, beat the eggs lightly. Add the bread crumbs, herbs, the remaining salt, and ⅛ teaspoon black pepper; blend well. Stir in the arugula mixture and a little more than half of the cheese.

3. Heat the remaining 2 tablespoons olive oil in the same pan over medium heat. Add the egg mixture and cook until the eggs are set on the bottom and around the edges, about 3 minutes. Sprinkle the remaining cheese over the top.

4. Place under the broiler 6 inches from the heat and broil just until the eggs are lightly set in the center, about 2 minutes. Serve hot or at room temperature.

3	tablespoons olive oil
1	red bell pepper, roasted (see page 33) and diced, or ¾ cup roasted pepper strips
1	cup lightly packed arugula, cut into ribbons
1	teaspoon balsamic or red wine vinegar
½	teaspoon salt
	Freshly ground black pepper
8	eggs
¼	cup coarse fresh bread crumbs
¼	cup minced fresh herbs, preferably a mix of basil, rosemary, parsley, and sage
3	ounces fresh mozzarella cheese, preferably buffalo mozzarella, cut into ½-inch dice

Vegetable Couscous, Hot or Not

Harissa, a North African condiment made from habañero peppers, is a powerful hot sauce that packs a mighty punch. It is often served alongside this classic Moroccan dish, so diners can be as brave as they please. Without harissa, this dish is a light and lovely ode to springtime, full of delicate tastes and textures.

MAKES:
4 servings

PREP:
15 minutes

COOK:
10 minutes

1   **cup couscous**

¾   **cup chicken stock or reduced-sodium canned broth**

¼   **cup dried currants**

¼   **cup olive oil**

¼   **cup pine nuts**

1   **medium zucchini, diced**

1   **medium red bell pepper, diced**

¾   **teaspoon ground cumin**

    Pinch of cinnamon

½   **teaspoon salt**

4   **scallions, sliced**

1   **(15-ounce) can garbanzo beans, rinsed and drained**

½   **cup fresh or tiny frozen peas, thawed**

    Cayenne

¼   **cup fresh lemon juice**

¼   **cup mixed minced fresh herbs, such as cilantro, mint, and basil**

    Harissa (recipe follows)

1 Place the couscous in a medium heatproof bowl. Bring the chicken stock to a boil and pour over the couscous. Add the currants, cover tightly, and let stand 10 minutes.

2 Meanwhile, heat 1 tablespoon of the olive oil in a large skillet over high heat. Add the pine nuts and cook, stirring often, until golden and fragrant, 2 to 3 minutes. Remove with a slotted spoon and set aside.

3 Heat another tablespoon of olive oil in the same pan. Add the zucchini, bell pepper, cumin, cinnamon, and ¼ teaspoon of the salt. Cook, stirring often, until the pepper begins to soften, 3 to 4 minutes. Add the scallions, garbanzo beans, peas, and cayenne to taste and cook just until heated through, 1 to 2 minutes. Remove from the heat and set aside.

4 Fluff the couscous mixture with a fork and add the remaining 1 tablespoon olive oil, ¼ teaspoon salt, and the lemon juice; mix lightly. Add the contents of the skillet and the herbs, and toss lightly. Serve hot or at room temperature. Pass the harissa on the side.

Harissa

Harissa can be made ahead, covered, and stored in the refrigerator for several weeks. This recipe yields about ½ cup.

1	medium garlic clove
3	habañero peppers
1	teaspoon grated orange zest
¼	cup olive oil
1	tablespoon fresh lemon juice
¼	teaspoon salt
⅛	teaspoon caraway seeds

1 In a small food processor or mini-chopper, mince the garlic, habañero peppers, and orange zest. Add the olive oil, lemon juice, salt, and caraway seeds, and mix well.

A staple of North African cuisine, **couscous** is tiny pellets of semolina. Once cooked, this versatile pasta may be served alongside savory main dishes, with milk as porridge, or as part of a salad with dressing. Packaged or bulk couscous is available in Middle Eastern markets and most supermarkets. Israeli couscous has larger pearls of toasted pasta.

The small, ivory-colored seeds extracted from the cones of several species of pine trees go by the name **pine nuts**. They are prized for their rich, slightly resinous flavor. Also called Indian nut, piñon, pignoli or pignolia, this high-fat nut comes from the inside of the pinecone, which generally must be heated to facilitate its removal. This labor-intensive process makes these nuts expensive. Pine nuts are sold in bulk in health-food stores, and packaged in many supermarkets.

White Beans with Prosciutto, Fennel & Fried Sage

*Heady with the aroma of sage set against a pungent backdrop of garlic and prosciutto,
this is rustic Italian cooking at its best. Serve hot in winter or at room temperature in summer,
with lots of bread—either a crusty loaf of Italian bread or a soft pillow of focaccia.
When time allows, use dried beans that have been soaked and cooked.
Otherwise, canned beans may be used, although they have a softer texture.*

MAKES:
3 to 4 servings

PREP:
15 minutes

COOK:
20 minutes

¼ cup olive oil

12 fresh sage leaves plus 3 tablespoons minced fresh sage

2 large garlic cloves, minced

¼ to ½ teaspoon crushed hot red pepper, to taste

1 medium onion, diced

1 small fennel bulb, trimmed and diced

2 ounces prosciutto, diced

4 cups cooked or 2 (15-ounce) cans navy or Great Northern beans, drained

½ cup ham stock or chicken broth

1 small roasted red bell pepper (see page 33), diced

⅓ cup fresh lemon juice

¾ teaspoon salt

1 In a large saucepan, heat the olive oil over high heat. Add the sage leaves and cook until crisped, 30 to 45 seconds. With a slotted spoon, transfer the sage to a paper towel.

2 Add the garlic and hot red pepper to the oil remaining in the saucepan and cook, stirring constantly, 30 seconds. Add the onion, fennel, and prosciutto and cook, stirring often, until the fennel softens, 4 to 5 minutes.

3 Add the beans and ham stock, reduce the heat to medium-low, and simmer, partially covered, until slightly thickened, 12 to 15 minutes. Stir in the roasted pepper, lemon juice, salt, and minced sage. Crumble the fried sage and sprinkle over the top.

Open-Faced Omelet Juliette

The vegetable mixture is borrowed from a rich and thoroughly satisfying side dish from France affectionately called **Pomme Juliette**. *With the addition of eggs, it is marvelously transformed into a casual main course.*

MAKES:
4 to 6 servings

PREP:
15 minutes

COOK:
25 minutes

1 In a large nonstick ovenproof skillet, melt the butter over medium-high heat. Add the potatoes, shallots, and bell pepper. Cook, stirring often, until the potatoes are crisp and lightly browned, 12 to 15 minutes.

2 Add the mushrooms, cabbage, parsley, thyme, marjoram, and half of the salt. Season with half the pepper. Cook, stirring, until the mushrooms are wilted, 4 to 5 minutes.

3 Preheat the broiler. In a medium bowl, whisk the eggs together with the remaining salt and pepper. Add to the skillet. Reduce the heat to medium and cook, stirring occasionally, until the eggs begin to set, about 2 minutes. Cover and cook until the eggs are softly set, 2 to 3 minutes longer.

4 Lightly brush the surface of the eggs with the vinegar and place under the broiler 4 to 6 inches from the heat. Broil just until the top begins to brown, 1 to 2 minutes. Serve hot or at room temperature.

4	tablespoons unsalted butter
1¼	cups diced cooked potatoes
2	small shallots, sliced paper thin
½	a medium red bell pepper, finely diced
6	fresh mushrooms, sliced
1	cup shredded cabbage, preferably Savoy
1	tablespoon minced parsley
1	teaspoon minced fresh thyme
1	teaspoon minced fresh marjoram
¾	teaspoon salt
¼	teaspoon freshly ground black pepper
8	large eggs
2	teaspoons balsamic vinegar

Rice Torte with Creamy Eggplant & Mushrooms

Forget everything you remember about the ho-hum molded rice dishes from the past. This one, based on a Florentine recipe, is stylish, even a little elegant, although it is well-suited to many kinds of meals, including casual ones. The rice forms a creamy foundation for an eggplant and mushroom compote that is slowly cooked to a sublime texture, then enlivened with a final additional of fresh basil. It can be served hot or at room temperature, making it a versatile solution for buffets or cook-ahead meals.

MAKES:
6 to 8 servings

PREP:
15 minutes

SOAK:
15 minutes

COOK:
1 hour, 35 minutes

STAND:
5 minutes to 2 hours

½ cup dried mushrooms, preferably porcini

2 cups arborio rice
4 cups vegetable broth or chicken broth
2 tablespoons unsalted butter

½ cup grated Romano cheese
¼ teaspoon freshly ground pepper

2 tablespoons olive oil
1 large garlic clove, minced
1 small leek (white part only), cleaned, trimmed, and chopped
1 medium onion, chopped

1 large eggplant, peeled and cut into ½-inch cubes (about 3 cups)

¼ cup heavy cream

2 tablespoons minced fresh basil
¼ teaspoon salt
Pinch of grated nutmeg, preferably fresh

3 tablespoons fine dry bread crumbs

1 Place the mushrooms in a small heatproof bowl and cover with ½ cup boiling water; let stand 15 minutes. Strain the mushrooms, reserving the liquid. Chop the mushrooms and set aside.

2 In a large saucepan, combine the rice, vegetable broth, and 1 tablespoon of the butter. Bring to a boil and reduce the heat to medium-low. Simmer gently, uncovered, stirring often, until the liquid is absorbed, 10 to 12 minutes. Remove from the heat and stir in the Romano cheese and pepper. Transfer the rice to a bowl and set aside. Wipe out the saucepan with a wet paper towel.

3 Heat the olive oil in the same saucepan. Add the garlic, leek, and onion and cook over medium heat, stirring occasionally, until the onion begins to soften, 4 to 5 minutes. Add the eggplant and the mushrooms with their liquid. Cover, reduce the heat to low, and cook until the eggplant is tender, 35 to 40 minutes, stirring in 1 tablespoon cream about every 10 minutes. (When fully cooked, the mixture should be creamy but not wet.) Add the basil, salt, nutmeg, and additional pepper to taste.

4 About 15 minutes before baking, preheat the oven to 425° F. Butter a 2½-quart soufflé dish or round casserole with the remaining 1 tablespoon butter, and sprinkle with the bread crumbs.

5 Place half of the reserved rice in the prepared baking dish and spread to form a smooth layer. Top with the vegetable mixture, then the remaining rice. Bake 30 minutes. The torte can be served hot or at room temperature. To serve hot, let stand 5 minutes, and then loosen from the sides with a small knife and invert onto a serving plate. To serve at room temperature, hold at room temperature for up to 2 hours. Loosen from the pan and invert onto a plate at serving time.

An Italian variety of rice, **arborio** has short, plump grains high in starch content which, when cooked, develop a creamy, sauce-like consistency ideal for risotto. Its grains are more diminutive and fatter than any other short-grain rice. You can buy arborio rice in Italian delicatessens and well-stocked food stores.

Risotto with Asparagus, Mushrooms & Smoked Trout

With its world-class status, risotto can intimidate some cooks just as much as it tantalizes. Its fearsome reputation for being hard to cook isn't fully justified. As long as a few simple steps are followed, it's very easy and the results sublime.

MAKES:
2 to 3 servings

PREP:
15 minutes

COOK:
30 minutes

2   **tablespoons unsalted butter**

1   **tablespoon olive oil**

½   **pound slender asparagus, trimmed and cut into 1-inch pieces**

½   **pound mixed wild mushrooms (such as cremini, shiitake, or morels), cut in half**

½   **teaspoon salt**

1   **large shallot, minced**

1   **cup arborio rice**

¼   **cup dry white wine**

3   **cups hot chicken stock or reduced-sodium canned broth**

1   **teaspoon minced fresh rosemary**

4   **ounces flaked smoked trout**
     Freshly ground pepper

1 In a large heavy saucepan, melt 1 tablespoon butter in the oil over high heat. Add the asparagus, mushrooms, and ¼ teaspoon salt. Cook, stirring, until the asparagus is crisp-tender, 3 to 4 minutes. Remove from the pan.

2 Melt the remaining 1 tablespoon butter in the same pan over medium-high heat. Add the shallot and cook, stirring often, until it begins to soften, 2 to 3 minutes. Add the rice and stir so it is well coated with the butter mixture. Pour in the wine and boil until most of the liquid is cooked away, about 3 minutes.

3 Add ¾ cup of hot chicken stock and reduce the heat to medium-low. Cook, stirring almost constantly, until the stock is almost absorbed. Add about ½ cup stock and the rosemary and continue cooking and stirring, adding more chicken stock as the mixture becomes dry. After about 15 minutes, most of the stock should have been added, and the rice should almost be tender.

4 Return the asparagus and mushrooms to the pan along with any remaining stock, the trout, the remaining ¼ teaspoon salt, and pepper to taste. Cook just until the mixture is creamy, 3 to 5 minutes. Serve at once.

Risotto Verde

A glorious abundance of broccoli and fennel melds into the creamy rice, only to be further gilded with Gorgonzola cheese. In this recipe, al dente applies only to the rice. For the most impact, the vegetables should be softly cooked so they break down and form a coarse puree that accents the creamy quality of risotto. Like all risottos, this one doesn't wait for diners; diners gladly wait for it.

MAKES:
3 to 4 servings

PREP:
15 minutes

COOK:
35 minutes

1 Place the fennel and broccoli in a large saucepan and add enough water to cover. Bring to a boil and cook until the vegetables are completely softened, 8 to 10 minutes. Drain well. When the vegetables are cool enough to handle, chop them finely.

2 Melt the butter in the same saucepan over medium heat. Add the onion and garlic and cook until the onion is softened, about 5 minutes. Add the rice and stir so it is well coated with butter. Increase the heat to high, add the wine, and boil until the wine is almost evaporated, about 3 minutes.

3 Reduce the heat to medium-low and add about ¾ cup of the hot stock. Cook, stirring almost constantly, until most of the stock has been absorbed. Continue adding stock in ½-cup portions, cooking and stirring until it is almost absorbed before adding more. When all of the stock has been added, the rice should be tender but still firm and a little creamy.

4 Add the vegetables, Gorgonzola, cream, thyme, and pepper. Cook to heat through, 2 to 3 minutes. Season with salt to taste. Sprinkle the Parmesan cheese on top.

1½ cups chopped fennel bulb
1½ cups chopped broccoli

2 tablespoons unsalted butter
1 small onion, finely diced
1 garlic clove, minced

1 cup arborio rice
⅓ cup dry white wine

3 cups hot chicken stock or reduced-sodium canned broth

¼ cup (1 ounce) crumbled Gorgonzola or other blue-veined cheese
2 tablespoons heavy cream
1 teaspoon minced fresh thyme leaves or a pinch of dried
¼ teaspoon freshly ground pepper

Salt
⅓ cup grated Parmesan cheese

RECIPE INDEX

Sausage, smoked
Chicken paprikash, 78
Italian chicken and sausage with rice and
  seared peppers, 80
Pasta paella, 142
White bean, chicken, and sausage cassoulet, 81

Sausage, spiced chicken or turkey
Chicken pot au feu, 84
Tortellini with sausage and pepper ragout, 150

Scallops
Italian fish stew with vinegar-glazed leeks
  and onions, 122
Pasta with scallops and salad greens in
  creamy tarragon dressing, 132
São Paulo seafood stew, 128
Scallops with corn, bacon, and tomatoes, 37
Seafood pasta primavera, 148

Shrimp
Asian-style shrimp, cabbage, and noodle
  sauté, 50
Crab, shrimp, and corn chowder, 19
Grecian Isles baked shrimp with feta and
  tomatoes, 125
Italian fish stew with vinegar-glazed leeks
  and onions, 122
Mongolian fire pot with beef and shrimp, 24
Pad Thai, 44
Pasta paella, 142
Seafood pasta primavera, 148
St. Peter street seafood and sausage gumbo, 12

Snap peas. See Peas, sugar snap

Snow peas. See Peas, snow

Spinach
Bleu black eyes with spinach and bacon, 171
Carrot couscous with ragout of spring
  vegetables, 157
Mongolian fire pot with beef and shrimp, 24
Persian rice cake with lamb and spinach, 110

Sprouts, bean
Madras-spiced lentils with spinach, 159
Pad Thai, 44
Transparent noodles with stir-fried turkey
  and asparagus, 48

Squash, butternut
Aztec vegetable stew with black beans and
  corn, 155
Carbonnade of root vegetables, 170
Winter squash with hominy and chilies, 166

Squash, chayote
Vegetable gumbo, 27

Squash, yellow
Chicken pot au feu, 84
Ratatouille boats with goat cheese, olives,
  and capers, 165
Ratatouille with poached eggs, 164

Squash, zucchini
Aztec vegetable stew with black beans and
  corn, 155
Baked tortellini, 151
Braised round steak with country garden
  vegetables, 92
Fish and vegetables with cilantro, 121
Gnocchi with wild mushroom broth, 135
Malaysian vegetable stew with gingery
  coconut milk, 168
Orzo with vegetable tomato sauce and
  pesto, 134
Ratatouille boats with goat cheese, olives,
  and capers, 165
Ratatouille with poached eggs, 164
Roasted vegetable stew, 61
Santa Fe chicken with black beans, corn, and
  poblanos, 32
Summer chicken and vegetable sauté, 47
Vegetable couscous, hot or not, 174
Vegetable gumbo, 27
Vegetable stew with turkey meatballs, 86

Swiss chard. See Chard, Swiss

Tomatillos
Green chili pork stew, 100

Tomatoes, fresh
Aztec vegetable stew with black beans and
  corn, 155
Basque-style chicken, 72
Bourbon-glazed ham steaks with snap pea
  succotash, 46
Braised chicken and vegetables with
  ginger-lime broth and couscous, 74

Chicken paprikash, 78
Chicken stew with rice and spring
  vegetables, 71
Eggplant and sausage stew, 105
Fish and vegetables with cilantro, 121
Grecian Isles baked shrimp with feta and
  tomatoes, 125
Gypsy goulash, 62
Lebanese chicken with bulgur salad, 38
Madras-spiced lentils with spinach, 159
Mexican-style rolled flank steak, 90
Mussels with chorizo, corn, and tomatoes, 129
Pasta shells with sausage in tomato-cream
  sauce, 146
Pasta with broccoli rabe and tomatoes, 131
Pasta with scallops and salad greens in
  creamy tarragon dressing, 132
Penne with tomatoes, mint, and sage, 141
Penne with white beans, chard, and
  anchovies, 144
Peruvian-spiced baked fish with quinoa, 68
Potato and celery root soup with apples and
  smoked trout, 23
Puebla-style burritos, 35
Ragout of fresh clams with artichokes and
  tomatoes, 138
Ratatouille boats with goat cheese, olives,
  and capers, 165
Ratatouille with poached eggs, 164
Red snapper creole, 124
Scallops with corn, bacon, and tomatoes, 37
Seafood pasta primavera, 148
Spring lamb navarin, 108
St. Peter street seafood and sausage gumbo, 12
Summer chicken and vegetable sauté, 47
Swordfish with artichokes, olives, and
  potatoes, 119
Tuna, broccoli, and Brie casserole, 67
Vegetable gumbo, 27
White bean, chicken, and sausage cassoulet, 81
Yucatán-style chicken soup with poblano
  pepper and lime, 14

Tomato sauce. See Sauce, tomato

Trout, smoked
Potato and celery root soup with apples and
  smoked trout, 23
Risotto with asparagus, mushrooms, and
  smoked trout, 180

Tuna
Sicilian tuna with fettuccine and melting
    onions, 126
Tuna, broccoli, and Brie casserole, 67

Turkey
Turkey breast with stewed barley and leek
    pilaf, 85
Turkey posole, 51

Turkey, ground
Andrew's ready spaghetti, 147
Transparent noodles with stir-fried turkey
    and asparagus, 48
Vegetable stew with turkey meatballs, 86

Turnips
Beef stew with the right attitude, 98
Carbonnade of root vegetables, 170
Chicken pot au feu, 84
Down Island chicken and turnip stew, 77
Malaysian vegetable stew with gingery
    coconut milk, 168

Veal
Gypsy goulash, 62
Moroccan veal tagine with orange and
    cumin, 112
Osso bucco, 116

Yellow squash. See Squash, yellow

Zucchini. See Squash, zucchini

FYI INDEX

Adobo sauce, 91
Allspice, 57
Anchovies, 145
Andouille sausage, 13
Annatto seeds, 69
Arborio rice, 179
Asparagus, 49
Balsamic vinegar, 153
Bean threads, 49
Béchamel sauce, 137
Boiling onions, 109
Boniato, 169
Bourbon, 59
Brussels sprouts, 57
Bulgur, 39
Cannellini beans, 17
Capers, 83
Cardamom, 111
Cayenne, 161
Cellophane noodles, 49
Chard, Swiss, 17
Chervil, 109
Chicken skin, stripping, 41
Chili oil, 25
Chili paste, 45
Chili powder, 87
Chipolte chili peppers, 91
Chorizo, 31
Cilantro, 31
Cinnamon, 75
Citrus zest, 41
Clams, 139
Corn kernels, removing, 107
Couscous, 175
Creole seasoning, 13
Endive, 133
Fish, white-fleshed, 69
Fish sauce, 45
Fresh herbs, mincing, 39
Frittata, 153
Ginger, 25
Hoisin sauce, 103
Jalapeño chili peppers, 41
Lasagna noodles, precooked, 137
Linguica sausage, 143
Marjoram, 73
Mint, 127

Meatballs, forming, 87
Navarin, 109
Olives, 73
Olives, pitting, 73
Orzo, 111
Pancetta, 17
Pappardelle, 149
Paprika, 79
Parmesan cheese, 145
Peppers, roasting, 33
Pine nuts, 147
Poblano peppers, 33
Port, 99
Precooked lasagna noodles, 137
Primavera, 149
Prunes, 95
Queso fresco, 107
Ragout, 139
Rice noodles, 145
Ricotta, 137
Roast peppers, 33
Saffron, 143
Scallops, 133
Serrano chili peppers, 91
Sesame seeds, 103
Sesame seeds, toasting, 103
Shallots, 113
Shallots, mincing, 113
Soft-shell crabs, 43
Soft-shell crabs, cleaning, 43
Stew meat, 95
Sun-dried tomatoes, 117
Sweet potatoes, 83
Swiss chard, 17
Trenette, 149
Tuna, 127
Vidalia onions, 59
Vinegar, 127
White-fleshed fish, 69

U.S. & Metric Liquid Equivalents

U.S. Teaspoons	U.S. Tablespoons	U.S. Cups	U.S. Fluid Ounces	Metric Milliliters
¼				1.3 spoons
½				2.5 spoons
1				5 spoons
3	1	1/16	½	15 spoons
	2	⅛	1	30
	3	⅙	1½	45
	4	¼	2	60
		⅓	2½	75
		⅜	3	90
		½	4	125
		⅔	5	150
		¾	6	175
		1	8	237
		1¼	10	300
		1½	12	355
		2 (1 pint)	16	473
		3	24	710
		4 (1 quart)	32	946
		5	40	1.1 liters
		6	48	1.4 liters
		8 (½ gallon)	64	1.9 liters
		16 (1 gallon)	128	3.8 liters

U.S. Dry & Canned Weight	Metric Dry & Canned Weight
¼ teaspoon	1.25 ml spoon
½ teaspoon	2.5 ml spoon
1 teaspoon	5 ml spoon
1 tablespoon	15 ml spoon
½ ounce	14.2 grams
1 ounce	28.3 grams
1½ ounces	42.5 grams
2 ounces	56.7 grams
2½ ounces	70.9 grams
3 ounces	84 grams
4 ounces	112 grams
5 ounces	140 grams
6 ounces	168 grams
7 ounces	196 grams
8 ounces	224 grams
10 ounces	280 grams
12 ounces	336 grams
14½ ounces	406 grams
15½ ounces	434 grams
16 ounces (1 pound)	448 grams
19 ounces	532 grams
24 ounces	672 grams
26 ounces	728 grams
28 ounces	784 grams
32 ounces (2 pounds)	896 grams
2½ pounds	1.1 kilograms
3 pounds	1.4 kilograms
4 pounds	1.8 kilograms
5 pounds	2.3 kilograms

Approximate Metric Equivalents for Some Common Ingredients

Breadcrumbs (dry)	1 cup	90 grams
Breadcrumbs (fresh)	1 cup	45 grams
Beans (dry)	2 cups	500 grams
Butter	1 tablespoon	15 grams
Cheese (grated Parmesan)	1 cup	100 grams
Cornstarch	1 tablespoon	10 grams
Flour (unsifted)	1 cup	142 grams
Meat, cooked (diced, shredded)	1 cup	150 grams
Raisins	1 cup	200 grams
Rice, orzo	1 cup	240 grams
Sugar	1 cup	240 grams

Oven Temperature Conversion Chart

°Fahrenheit	°Celsius	Gas Mark
250	130	½
275	140	1
300	150	2
325	160/170	3
350	180	4
375	190	5
400	200	6
425	210/220	7
450	230	8
475	240	9

U.S. Lengths (inch/inches)	Metric Lengths (centimeter/centimeters)
¼	0.6
½	1.3
¾	1.9
1	2.5
1¼	3.2
1½	3.8
2	5
5	12.7
10	25.4